GLOUCESTER MASSACHUSETTS

ROCKPORT PUBLISHERS

the **Craft Painting Sourcebook**

a guide to beautiful patterns on 47 everyday surfaces

the

ROCKPORT

Portions of this book have previously been published by Rockport Publishers, Inc., in *Ceramic Painting Color Workshop* (© 2001 by Rockport Publishers, Inc.), by Doreen Mastandrea; in *Painted Furniture* (© 2001 by Rockport Publishers, Inc.), by Virginia Patterson and Francine Hornberger; in *Painting Glass with the Color Shaper* (© 2001 by Paula DeSimone), by Paula DeSimone; and in *Decorative Painter's Color Shaper Book* (© 1999 by Paula De Simone) by Paula De Simone.

First published in the United States of America by
Rockport Publishers, Inc.
33 Commercial Street
Gloucester, Massachusetts 01930-5089
Telephone: (978) 282-9590
Fax: (978) 283-2742
www.rockpub.com

Library of Congress Cataloging-in-Publication data available

ISBN 1-56496-924-X

10 9 8 7 6 5 4 3 2 1

Grateful acknowledgment is given to Paula DeSimone for her work on pages 74-127, 136-137, and 182-237; to Francine Hornberger for her work on pages 130-135, 138-179, and 256-267; to Doreen Mastandrea for her work on pages 10-71 and 240-255; to Livia McRee for her work on pages 10-71 and 240-255; and to Virginia Patterson for her work on pages 130-135, 138-179, and 256-267.

Cover Image: DW Design, London

Printed in Singapore

contents

| the craft painting sourcebook

introduction

Deciding how to decorate your craft project can be an overwhelming prospect for crafters who do not necessarily consider themselves painters. What to paint and how to approach a project are things that many crafters struggle with.

Whether working on glass, ceramic, wood, or metal, this collection is the ultimate sourcebook for paints, palettes, and patterns for all of your craft projects. More than 40 projects, with easy step-by-step instructions featuring inspired use of materials, show you how to create unique patterns and palettes for a range of decorative items. Learn how to paint an Art Nouveau glass candleholder, sgrafitto ceramics, and French country–style furniture.

This is a complete craft painting course in a book. It will help you transform your craft projects into works of art. This book will not only provide you with great project ideas but will help you choose the right materials, color palettes, and patterns for your projects. Go ahead and paint!

painting ceramics

Painting on ceramics, unlike painting on canvas, presents the additional element of form. Certain colors and designs will accentuate particular ceramic forms, so making thoughtful choices when planning a project creates artful, as well as useful, ceramic pieces.

When planning a project, always keep in mind that ceramics are meant to be used. Consider how, where, and with what the piece will be used. Consider, for example, the time of day the piece will be used; whether it will stay indoors or outdoors; and whether it will be used in a celebratory or reflective setting. Planning colors and designs accordingly will enhance the beauty of any piece.

Deciding how to use colors in painting can be overwhelming, given the wide variety of hues. Color preferences are, above all, personal, so when selecting a palette, consider the mood and feeling it evokes in you. The colors of each palette presented in this guide work together to convey a specific look and feel and offer a sure starting point.

Colors For Your Every Mood

FAVORITE BRIGHT COLORS

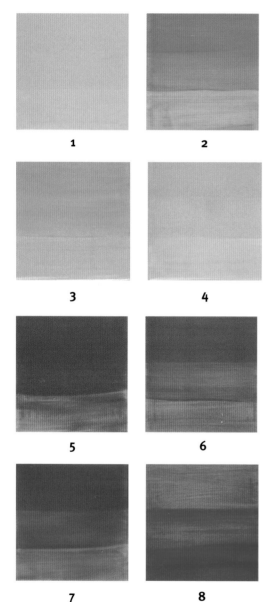

1 bright yellow

2 lime green

3 orange

4 honey yellow

5 apple red

6 deep orange

7 aquamarine

8 turquoise

The exciting colors of this palette lend the intensity of summer to a project. Sunny days, picnics, ripened fruit, and flowers bursting with color come to mind. Imagine a heap of tantalizing, vibrantly colored fruits...and a bowl large enough to accommodate the whole bunch! Red, ripe strawberries nestled in a turquoise or lime green bowl will look stunning and electrified.

A combination of colors from this palette—like orange, apple red, and lime green—can spark a traditional Mexican spirit. Pieces such as chip-n-dip plates, and platters that are intended to be used at gatherings, summertime celebrations, and parties look vibrant and festive when done in bright colors.

Wake up to these energizing colors! They can help start the day, making them the perfect choices for a coffee mug. The daily morning routine can also be a personal, reflective time. Try images on mugs that evoke a fond memory or a favorite hobby, to impart a cheery mood to the day or to spark creativity.

FAVORITE COOL COLORS

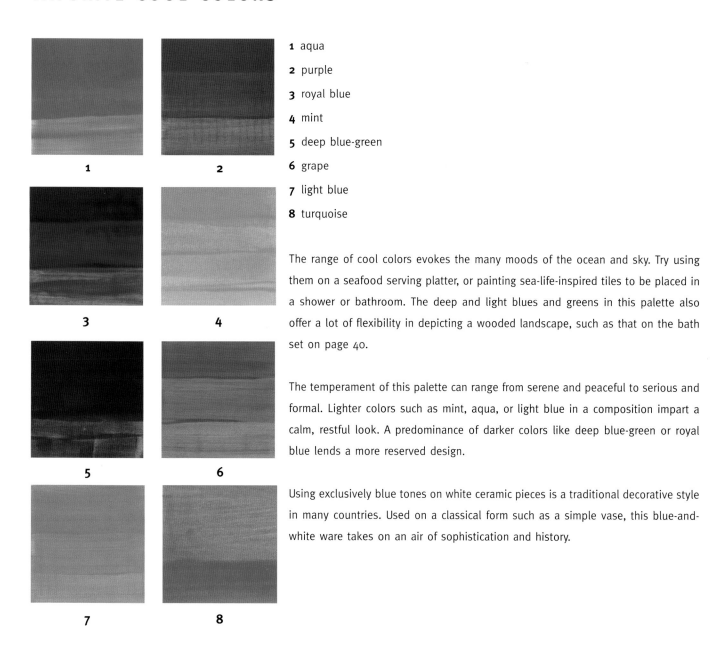

1 aqua

2 purple

3 royal blue

4 mint

5 deep blue-green

6 grape

7 light blue

8 turquoise

The range of cool colors evokes the many moods of the ocean and sky. Try using them on a seafood serving platter, or painting sea-life-inspired tiles to be placed in a shower or bathroom. The deep and light blues and greens in this palette also offer a lot of flexibility in depicting a wooded landscape, such as that on the bath set on page 40.

The temperament of this palette can range from serene and peaceful to serious and formal. Lighter colors such as mint, aqua, or light blue in a composition impart a calm, restful look. A predominance of darker colors like deep blue-green or royal blue lends a more reserved design.

Using exclusively blue tones on white ceramic pieces is a traditional decorative style in many countries. Used on a classical form such as a simple vase, this blue-and-white ware takes on an air of sophistication and history.

FAVORITE SOFT COLORS

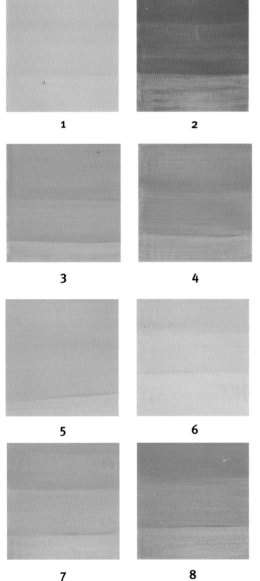

1   **1** pale yellow

2 pink

3 peach

4 lavender

5 beige

6 light pink

7 mint

8 periwinkle

Soft colors are non-intrusive, so these are the colors to choose for a restful, soothing, and quiet setting.

Dessert plates showing off white frosted or powdered desserts look luscious, and a tea set for one invites quiet contemplation. A light switch like the one on page 60 blends easily into a room's décor and adds a creative accent against a white wall.

The muted look of soft colors can also create a feeling of age or antiquity. Think of a faded frescoed wall or a sun-bleached outdoor mural. To recreate this feeling, try sponging or layering paints for a variegated depth of color.

TIP: When sponging colors it is best to use colors of similar intensity so they blend well together. Avoid using very dark colors with very light colors—the light colors will get lost.

FAVORITE EARTH COLORS

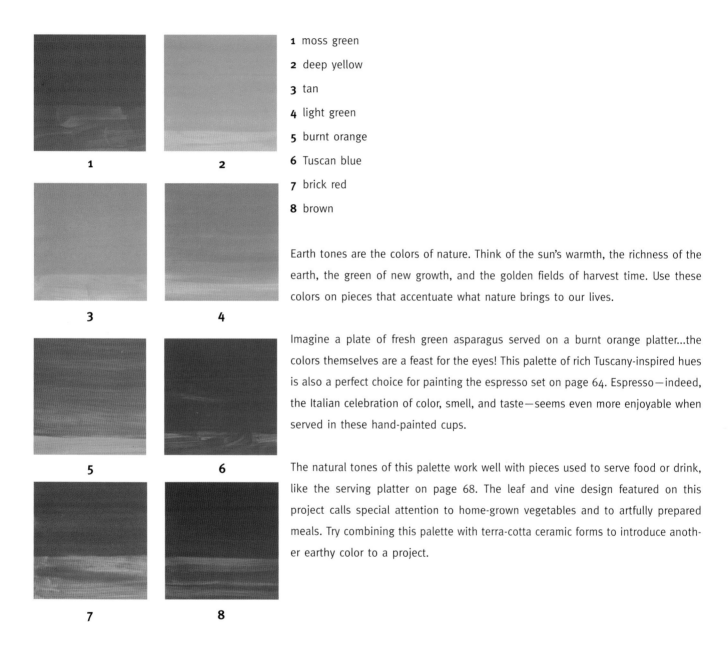

1 moss green

2 deep yellow

3 tan

4 light green

5 burnt orange

6 Tuscan blue

7 brick red

8 brown

Earth tones are the colors of nature. Think of the sun's warmth, the richness of the earth, the green of new growth, and the golden fields of harvest time. Use these colors on pieces that accentuate what nature brings to our lives.

Imagine a plate of fresh green asparagus served on a burnt orange platter...the colors themselves are a feast for the eyes! This palette of rich Tuscany-inspired hues is also a perfect choice for painting the espresso set on page 64. Espresso—indeed, the Italian celebration of color, smell, and taste—seems even more enjoyable when served in these hand-painted cups.

The natural tones of this palette work well with pieces used to serve food or drink, like the serving platter on page 68. The leaf and vine design featured on this project calls special attention to home-grown vegetables and to artfully prepared meals. Try combining this palette with terra-cotta ceramic forms to introduce another earthy color to a project.

the craft painting sourcebook

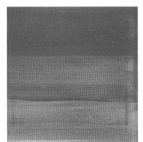

illustrated MUGS

Here, a single bright background color calls attention to the crisp, modern, black-and-white designs on these mugs rather than competes with them. A whole set, each painted with a different bright hue, energizes the breakfast table no matter what you're drinking. Try designing the motifs for each mug around a central theme such as geometric shapes, letters, or numbers.

MATERIALS

- **#3 or #4 round brush**
- **thin liner brush**
- **masking tape**
- **pencil**
- **ceramic paint underglaze colors: lime green, deep orange, black**

STARTING OUT
Masking tape creates quick, perfect templates for the rectangles and stripes on these mugs. When drawing small-scale designs, avoid adding details. Keep the designs simple to create maximum impact.

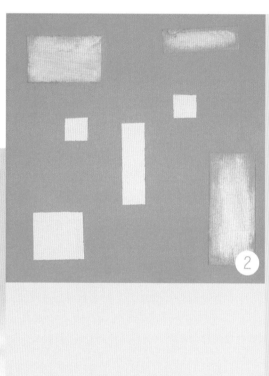

STEP 1 Pencil in two lines about ¼" (.5 cm) apart just under the lip of the mug. Draw one line on the inside of the cup about as far down as the bottom line on the outside. Tape equally spaced stripes on the handles of the mug. Cut a few rectangles of varying sizes from the tape and apply them randomly around the mug.

STEP 2 Paint three coats of deep orange or lime green on the mug under the bottom pencil lines, inside and out, excluding the handle. Let each coat dry completely before applying the next one. Remove the tape from the mug once it has dried. If any paint has bled under the taped areas, carefully scrape it away using a craft knife.

tip

If you find it awkward to tape the handle and you don't have difficulty staying within the lines when you paint, try drawing the stripes freehand in pencil.

tip

Keep line drawings simple. They are easy to paint and are bold rather than busy.

STEP 3 Pencil in designs in each of the white rectangles created by the tape. Using a thin liner brush, paint over all pencil lines with one coat of black. Any pencil lines that remain visible will burn off in the kiln. Paint around the taped stripes on the handle with one coat of black. Remove the tape. If necessary, scrape away excess paint with a craft knife, or add paint with a small brush to ensure crisp lines. Patterns for this project can be found on page 240.

variation

VARIATION

Wide, alternating stripes of color are vivid enough to stand alone. Here, the linear design is maintained by continuing the stripes to the handle.

Pencil in two lines about 1/4" (.5 cm) apart just under the lip of the mug. Below them, draw two lines around the mug to create three equal sections. Draw two lines around the handle to create a visually continuous stripe pattern. Apply three coats of deep orange on the inside of the mug, continuing outward to the second line under the lip. In each of the remaining striped areas, apply three coats of one color. Bright yellow, aquamarine, and lime green were used for the stripes on this mug. Using a thin liner brush, paint over pencil lines with one coat of black.

DEEP ORANGE

BRIGHT YELLOW

AQUAMARINE

LIME GREEN

salt & pepper SHAKERS

MATERIALS

- **#3 or #4 round brush**
- **thin liner brush**
- **pencil**
- **ceramic paint underglaze colors: lime green, bright yellow, apple red, black**

These nature-themed shakers will add a touch of whimsy to the table. A matching set is created not only by using related motifs, but also by repeating the same three colors in both shakers. The leaves are a combination of bright yellow and lime green with a background of apple red, while the flowers are bright yellow and apple red with a background of lime green. A simple shift in the dominant color makes each shaker unique but harmonious.

STARTING OUT To transfer designs more easily to a curved surface, try cutting the tracing pattern out of adhesive vinyl. It can be easily removed from or repositioned on ceramic surfaces.

STEP 1 Cut out the leaf template on page 241 and trace the pattern randomly around the shaker with a pencil. Then draw a line down the center of each leaf. Cut out the flower template on page 244 and trace this pattern randomly around the other shaker with a pencil.

STEP 2 Paint each leaf with two coats of lime green. Paint one coat of bright yellow over half of each leaf. Let each coat dry completely before applying the next one. Paint each flower with two coats of bright yellow. When completely dry, dip the handle end of your brush in apple red and make a dot in the center of each flower. Use enough paint on the handle end to create a solid dot. Too little paint will cause unevenly colored, incomplete, or translucent dots after firing.

tip

With a little practice, you can draw simple patterns, such as these, freehand to save time.

VARIATION

This shaker incorporates a traditional Italian scroll pattern, reminiscent of a curving vine.

Draw the leaves on the shaker as indicated in step 1 of the main projecte. Draw a freehand wave pattern around the neck of the shaker with a line above and below it. Paint the leaves as indicated. Paint the entire background except for the neck of the shaker with three coats of turquoise. Paint the wave pattern with apple red and green. Here, equal parts bright yellow and turquoise were mixed to create a new green. Using a thin liner brush, outline the wave pattern and the leaves with one coat of black. Also paint the scroll pattern in black. Finally, paint dots of apple red at the curled end of each scroll.

(3)

STEP 3 Paint the remaining areas of the leaf shaker with three coats of brick red, carefully avoiding the leaves. Let each coat dry completely before applying the next one. Using a thin liner brush, outline and paint a line down the middle of each leaf with one coat of black. Paint the remaining areas of the flower shaker with three coats of lime green, carefully avoiding the flowers. Outline the flowers, including the center circle, with one coat of black.

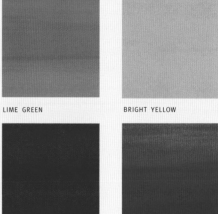

LIME GREEN

BRIGHT YELLOW

APPLE RED

TURQUOISE

the craft painting sourcebook

chip 'n dip
PARTY PLATTER

This feisty platter is sure to add a festive air to any party or gathering. Bright colors and free-form designs work together to create an energetic, informal mood. To create this design, adhesive vinyl was cut and adhered to the painted platter, making it easy to neatly paint the second color around the pattern. If the paint is completely dry, the vinyl won't damage it when removed.

MATERIALS

- **#3 or #4 round brush**
- **thin liner brush**
- **adhesive vinyl**
- **pencil**
- **ceramic paint underglaze colors: lime green, bright yellow, apple red, turquoise, white, black**

STARTING OUT

To make the abstract designs on this platter, sketch and cut out the design on paper first and adjust it as necessary. When you are happy with the pattern, trace it with a permanent marker on a piece of adhesive vinyl.

STEP 1 Paint one outer segment of the plate and the center with two coats of bright yellow. Paint another segment with two coats of lime green. Paint the final segment with two coats of turquoise. Be sure to leave the dividers and outer edge of the plate unpainted for now. Draw abstract designs freehand on adhesive vinyl, cut them out, and adhere them to the bottom of each outer segment. Make sure the paint is completely dry before trying to adhere the vinyl, or the adhesive won't stick.

STEP 2 Apply two coats of lime green over the bright yellow; two coats of turquoise over the lime green; and two coats of bright yellow over the turquoise. After each two applications, remove the vinyl when the paint is dry. Paint a circle of turquoise around the center section, leaving the middle yellow. Paint an apple red spiral in the yellow center.

tip

To create an outlined design like the one seen here in the green segment, simply cut out the center of the vinyl, roughly following the outer shape.

tip

If any paint has bled underneath the vinyl, gently scrape it away with a craft knife. Then, with a thin liner brush touch up the edges of the patterns to create a crisp edge where there may have been color bleeding.

STEP 3 Paint the outer edge, the underside of the plate, and the dividers of the plate with one generous coat of black. When the paint is completely dry, dip the handle end of your brush in white and dab dots of varying sizes all over the outer edge of the plate. The variation in dot size makes for a more intersting and active border. Use enough paint on the handle end to create a solid dot. Too little paint will cause unevenly colored, incomplete, or translucent dots after firing.

VARIATION

This plate is a fun way to present tortilla chips and salsa. Begin by painting the outer segments with three coats of apple red, orange, and deep orange as seen here. Using the template on page 243, draw a chili pepper in the center of the plate and paint the top lime green and the bottom apple red. Carefully outline the pepper in black, leaving a scalloped edge. Paint the dividers and center just to the scalloped edge with three coats of lime green. When the paint is completely dry, dip the handle end of your brush in apple red and mark a dot within each scallop of the border. Paint the outer edge with lime green and honey yellow stripes, alternating the widths as seen here. Outline the stripes with black.

LIME GREEN

ORANGE

HONEY YELLOW

APPLE RED

DEEP ORANGE

fruit
PLATES

MATERIALS

- #3 or #4 round brush
- thin liner brush
- ceramic paint underglaze
  colors: apple red, lime
  green, honey yellow,
  white, black

Sgraffito is an ancient ceramic carving technique that enables you to draw designs in paint. In this project, contrasting colors are layered, and a leaf pattern is carved into the top coat to reveal the black base coat. For maximum impact, the base coat must be solid and opaque. At least two top layers of paint are needed so that the top color remains distinct. In this case, three top layers of paint are used since the base coat is black.

STARTING OUT
Practice the sgraffito technique on a tile first. The final coat of paint should be wet, but not too wet, when carving the outline of the leaf. If it is too dry, the paint will chip off, leaving a messy look to the line.

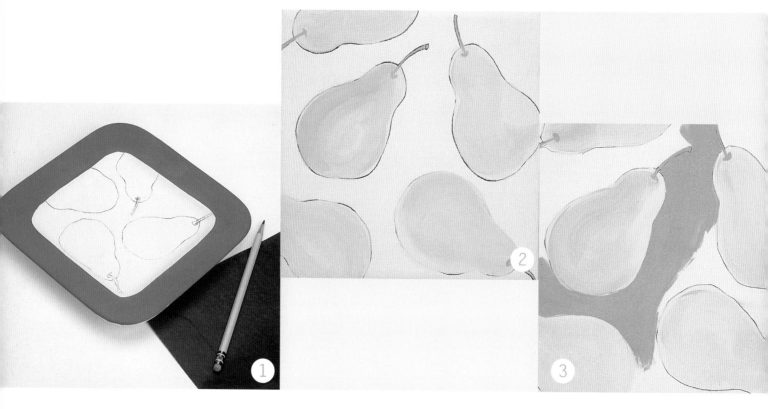

STEP 1 Transfer the pear design from page 242 several times to the center of the plate by using graphite paper or by tracing a cutout pear with a pencil. Arrange the pears in a random pattern, with some of the pears partially hidden by the edge of the plate. Paint the edge of the plate with two coats of black.

STEP 2 Paint the pears with one coat of honey yellow. While the paint is still wet, highlight the edges of the pears with a small amount of apple red, making sure the colors are well blended. Next, mix an equal amount of apple red and honey yellow to create the brown color for the stems. Paint the stems with two coats of the brown using a liner brush.

STEP 3 Paint around the pears with three coats of apple red. Let each coat dry completely before applying the next one. With a thin liner brush, outline the pears and stems with one coat of black. At the base of each stem, make the outline slightly thicker to suggest an indentation.

tips

To paint other fruit, such as the cherries seen in this project, use the same techniques as used for the pears, but be sure to pick background colors that will make the fruit stand out.

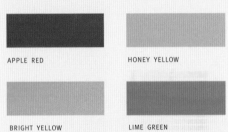

VARIATION 1 *To make this fruit bowl, use the same techniques described for the plate, but for the lemons paint over a bright yellow base coat with honey yellow, leaving some small areas of bright yellow as highlights. Using a thin liner brush, outline the lemons with one coat of black, and randomly add tiny dots to suggest a dimpled surface. Paint the black border on the outside of the bowl, and mix equal parts of apple red and white paint to create the lighter shade of the bowl's exterior.*

APPLE RED	HONEY YELLOW
BRIGHT YELLOW	LIME GREEN

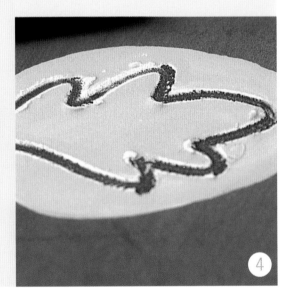

④

STEP 4 Paint oval shapes around the edge of the plate with one coat of white and let dry completely. Next, paint two coats of lime green over the white ovals. Let the first coat dry completely. While the second coat is still wet, take the end of a brush or a dull pencil and scrape the leaf outline into the paint so that the black base coat is revealed. Use a soft brush to remove any excess paint; wait until the piece is dry to avoid damaging the sgrafitto lines.

VARIATION 2 *With the plate at a diagonal, draw two lines to divide the space into three approximately equal parts. Then draw two more lines equally spaced and perpendicular to the first set of lines. Paint the sections with three coats of deep orange, lime green, and aquamarine as seen here. Finally, paint the lines between the sections with black.*

DEEP ORANGE	AQUAMARINE
LIME GREEN	

the craft painting sourcebook

stamped SEA TILES

Cool colors are the key to creating the aquatic complexion of these tiles. A background wash of color lends an ocean feel. The realistic motifs are stamped on the tiles, giving the impression of a detailed, framed print with relative ease.

MATERIALS

- **#3 or #4 round brush**
- **thin liner brush**
- **pencil**
- **fish stamp**
- **ceramic paint underglaze colors: light blue, royal blue, deep blue-green, aqua, black**

stamped
SEA TILES

STARTING OUT Both flexible foam and rubber stamps can be used with ceramic paints. Be sure to do a test stamping on a piece of paper first to see how much paint is necessary.

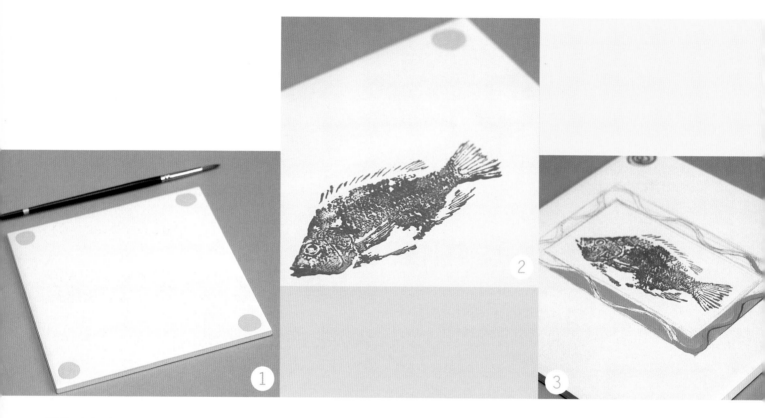

STEP 1 Paint the tile with one coat of light blue. Paint a dot in each corner, about the size of a dime, with one coat of aqua.

STEP 2 Brush an even coat of black paint on the stamp. Center the stamp on the tile and apply firm, even pressure.

STEP 3 With a pencil, draw a frame around the stamp. Paint the frame with one coat of royal blue. When it is completely dry, paint a freehand scalloped border in the frame with 2 coats of deep blue-green. See page 244 for patterns.

LIGHT BLUE

DEEP BLUE-GREEN

AQUA

ROYAL BLUE

VARIATION 1: This scrolling vine design works well independently. However, it becomes more intriguing when several of these tiles are placed next to each other as a bathroom backsplash. Paint a thin wash of light blue over the entire tile. Brush a coat of black paint on the stamp and press in the center of the tile. Draw a rectangular frame around the fish. Paint the inside of the frame with one coat of royal blue. Draw a freehand scroll within the confines of the frame border and paint it deep blue-green. Draw a larger scrolling vine pattern around the inside edge as shown in the template on page 246. Paint with a mix of deep blue-green and royal blue. Outline the frame, the inner scroll, and the outer scroll with one coat of black using a thin liner brush.

STEP 4 Using a thin liner brush, paint spirals in the corner circles with one coat of black. Outline the frame and scalloped border with black.

LINDA MASTANDREA

GRAPE

MINT

ROYAL BLUE

VARIATION 2: Conjure up your own whimsical creatures based on the unusual shapes and expressive eyes and mouths of sea animals or use the template on page 244. Pencil in animals and abstract shapes to suggest water. Paint the animals with one coat of mint, leaving the lips and eyes unpainted. Paint the abstract shapes with one thin coat of grape to achieve the translucent effect, and paint two heavy coats of royal blue to achieve the darker, opaque effect. Try using other color combinations such as aqua and deep blue-green for a bolder effect. Outline the animals and paint dots for the eyes in black.

two-tone
BOTTLE VASE

MATERIALS

- #0 or #1 and #5 or #6 round brushes
- thin liner brush
- ceramic paint underglaze colors: royal blue; deep blue-green; light blue; yellow for flower centers

This vase is reminiscent of the blue-and-white ware found throughout the history of world ceramics, from Ming vases to Wedgwood dinnerware. Two subtly different shades of blue add depth to the design and accentuate the voluptuous base, while the repeating graphic pattern creates a modern look. Experiment with the size of the flowers to see the variety of effects that can be achieved from a simple change in size. For example, a multitude of tiny flowers has a much daintier feel than a few large '70s-style blossoms. Use the templates on page 247 as guides.

STARTING OUT
The beauty and appeal of this vase lie in its luscious, rich color. Apply at least three solid, even coats of paint so that brush strokes are minimal.

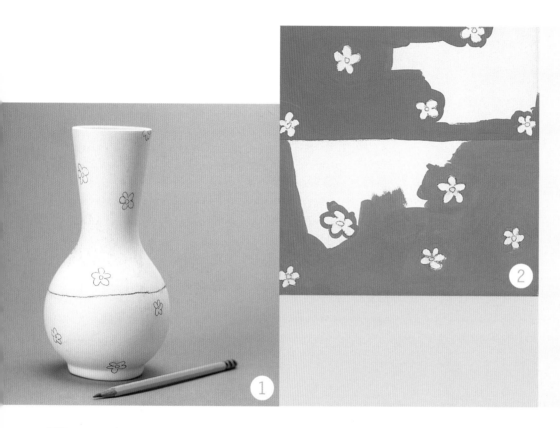

STEP 1 Draw a line around the vase about two-thirds of the way down from the top with a pencil. Draw freehand flowers, or transfer the flower from the pattern on page 247 randomly around the vase.

STEP 2 Paint the top part of the vase with at least three coats of royal blue, carefully avoiding the flowers. In the same manner, paint the bottom half of the vase with three coats of deep blue-green.

tip
To paint around the flowers easily, use a small round brush such as a #0 or #1 and only cover the area immediately surrounding each flower. Then, paint the remaining areas of the vase with a #5 or #6 round brush.

variations

VARIATION 1

Follow step 1 of the main project, but transfer the tri-leaf pattern from page 254 to the lower one-third of the vase. Paint the top of the vase as indicated in the main project. On the lower section, paint the leaves with one or two coats of mint or pale yellow. Let them dry completely. Using a thin liner brush, outline the leaves and add veins in black.

ROYAL BLUE	LIGHT BLUE
MINT	PALE YELLOW

STEP 3 Using a thin liner brush, add accent lines to the petals and outline the inner circle of the flowers with pale blue. With the blunt end of a brush, dab a dot of yellow in the center of each flower.

VARIATION 2

The vase seen here has a more classic blue-and-white ware look. Follow the directions for the main project, but paint the entire vase with royal blue and choose larger flowers.

ROYAL BLUE	LIGHT BLUE YELLOW FOR FLOWER CENTERS

landscape
BATHROOM SET

A bathroom always feels more comfortably intimate and relaxing when filled with blues and greens. This decorative but utilitarian set is sure to earn the admiration of guests and conjure up visions of beautiful, natural vistas. Painted in part with sponges, simple suggestive shapes and layers of paint are used to convey a moody sky and a forest scene. Experiment with the different types of sponges available at art and craft supply stores; try cutting them into specialized shapes to further refine the basic sponging technique.

MATERIALS

- **#4 or #5 round brush**
- **sea sponges or silk sponges**
- **ceramic paint underglaze colors: aqua; light blue; royal blue; mint; grape**

STARTING OUT

To successfully create an impressionistic landscape using sponging techniques, don't be afraid to wipe away paint or add additional layers. Since the loose style of this design makes a pattern impractical, use these directions for inspiration and guidance—experiment on a tile first, until you achieve the feeling of a landscape.

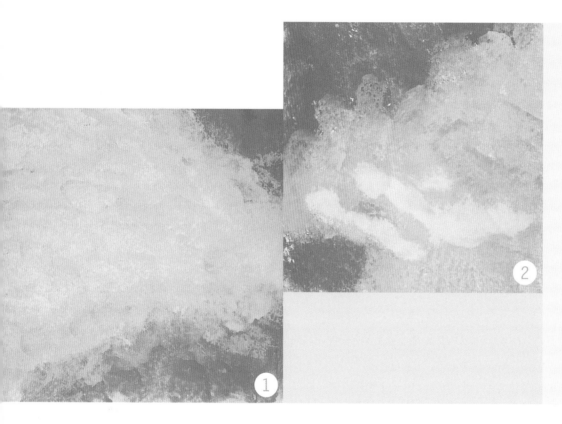

STEP 1 Sponge the entire surface of the cup, soap dish, and toothbrush holder with light blue. Using royal blue and then grape, sponge small areas of the sky and define a "ground line," which will determine where to begin sponging the bottom of the trees. Since royal blue and grape are the darkest colors used in this project, they are the most effective in visually separating the sky and the ground.

STEP 2 Using a clean sponge and water, wipe all the way down to the white clay body to create clouds. Don't worry about wiping off too much because more paint can be sponged on later.

(3)

STEP 3 With aqua, create trees with a #4 or #5 round brush, using short dabs for brush strokes. Lightly brush over some of the aqua with mint to add highlights and depth to the foliage. Finally, shade the ground area around the bases of the trees using royal blue and grape.

variation

VARIATION

Try adding another dimension to the landscape by applying a sgrafitto technique. Use a blunt pencil tip or the end of a brush to carve accent strokes that will add movement and vitality to your trees.

AQUA

LIGHT BLUE

ROYAL BLUE

MINT

GRAPE

fishbone
PLATTER

An oval platter was chosen to emphasize the elongated shape of this stylized fish skeleton. When a design, such as this one, demands a central motif that is solidly and evenly black, two coats of black are recommended. To properly contrast this dark, bold design, three heavy coats of paint were necessary to achieve maximum color intensity for the background and edge of the platter.

MATERIALS

- **wide, flat brush**
- **#3 or #4 round brush**
- **thin liner brush**
- **pencil**
- **ceramic paint underglaze colors: mint, grape, black**

STARTING OUT Be sure to select a ceramic form that can be proportionately filled by the fish skeleton. If necessary, adjust the overall size of the pattern to better fit the space.

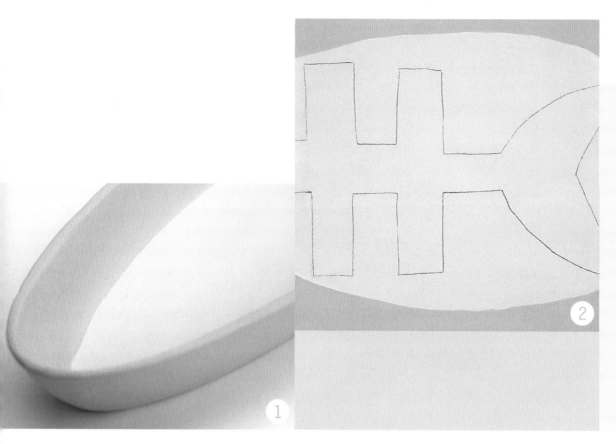

STEP 1 Using a wide, flat brush, apply three coats of mint to the bottom of the platter. Apply three coats of grape to the rim and the underside of the platter. Let each coat dry completely before applying the next one.

STEP 2 Transfer the fish skeleton pattern on page 245 to the inside bottom of the platter.

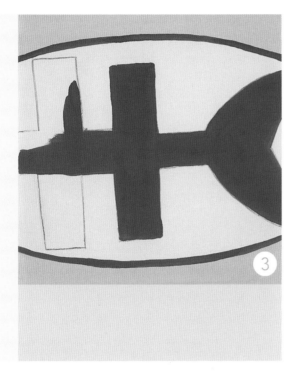

STEP 3 Fill in the fish with two coats of black for solid, even coverage. Outline with black the edge of the platter and the bottom where the mint and grape sections meet.

VARIATION

Transfer the wave border pattern on page 246 to the edge of the platter. Paint the inside of the platter just to the edge of the border pattern with two coats of light blue. Paint the border and the underside of the platter with three coats of royal blue. Let each coat dry completely before applying the next one. Next, transfer the starfish pattern on page 246 to the platter. Try adding a number of starfish of varying sizes. Mix equal parts light blue and royal blue, and paint the starfish with one coat of the mixture. With a thin liner brush, outline and add details to the starfish, as illustrated here, with royal blue.

LIGHT BLUE   ROYAL BLUE

the craft painting sourcebook

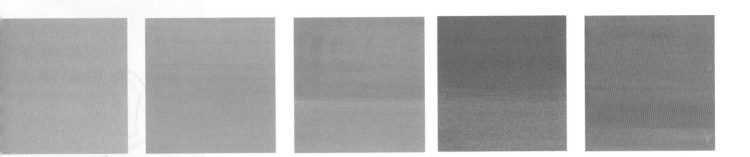

nestled
TEAPOT & CUP

This nestled tea-for-one set presents a unique design opportunity. Consider how each piece will look both separately and together while transferring the pattern. For this intimate ceramic form, a relaxed, washed effect was created by painting just two coats of an uplifting pastel yellow. The illusion of unused tea bags is created using a realistic light beige. As a variation, try painting the words on the tags in lowercase or script.

MATERIALS

- #3 or #4 round brush
- thin liner brush
- ceramic paint underglaze colors: pale yellow, beige, mint, periwinkle, peach, black

STARTING OUT Be sure to nestle the pot, lid, and cup together before transferring the pattern. Both handles should be aligned as well, to ensure the continuity of the design.

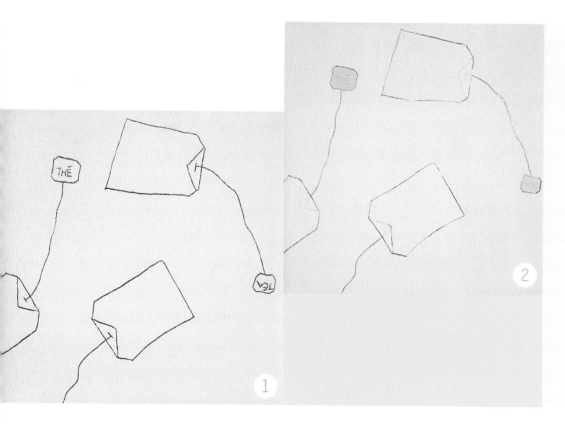

STEP 1 Paint the outside of the teapot and the entire cup with two coats of pale yellow. Transfer or copy the designs from page 248 on all sides in a random pattern. Technique is demonstrated on a tile here to better show fine detail.

STEP 2 Apply two coats of beige on the inside of each teabag. Paint the top folds of the teabags with three coats of beige to make them realistically darker. Paint each tag a different color, using two coats of mint, periwinkle, or peach. Let the paint dry completely.

tip
To simplify the process, transfer the tea bag pattern but not the string or tag. Then, draw in the strings and tags freehand. Don't forget: pencil lines will disappear during the firing process, so don't worry about mistakes.

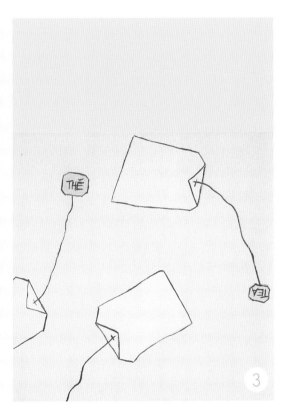

STEP 3 With a thin liner brush, paint in the strings and outline the tea bags and tags with black. Paint the word TEA on the tags or the names of your favorite varieties.

VARIATION

White, which enhances soft colors, is used here to create a daisy-like flower pattern. Paint a grid over the entire teapot with two coats of periwinkle. Then paint the grid's squares using two coats of mint, peach and/or pale yellow as seen here. Make sure the teapot's spout is within a square so that it can be painted with one color. Paint flowers with two coats of white in some of the squares and on the top of the teapot lid. Paint a pale yellow center in each flower.

PERIWINKLE

PEACH

MINT

PALE YELLOW

special occasion PLATES

Commemorative plates are the perfect outlet for a painter's creativity. Whether for a wedding, birth, graduation, anniversary, or other special event, the understated elegance of soft colors provides all the variety necessary to create tasteful, fun, personalized projects. The nearly flat surface allows maximum flexibility and ease in executing your designs, so don't be afraid to try something challenging.

MATERIALS

- **#4 round brush or ½" flat brush**
- **thin liner brush**
- **pencil**
- **ceramic paint underglaze colors: periwinkle, beige, peach, pale yellow, mint, lavender, white, black**

STARTING OUT

Take a look at stamps from different countries to glean ideas for personalizing this project. Stamps come in many different shapes and perforation styles, and the wide variety can inspire unusual designs.

STEP 1 Using a wide, flat brush, apply two coats of periwinkle over the entire plate, front and back. When completely dry, pencil in several rectangular shapes in a random pattern. With a round or flat brush, apply two good coats of white in the rectangles.

STEP 2 Pencil in a scalloped border around the white rectangles, using a postage stamp as a guide or the patterns on page 249. Draw a smaller inner rectangle within the stamps to create a border. Paint the scallops with two coats of periwinkle.

tip

Underglaze pencil smudges easily, so be careful not to handle the plate too much once this step is completed. (See variation.)

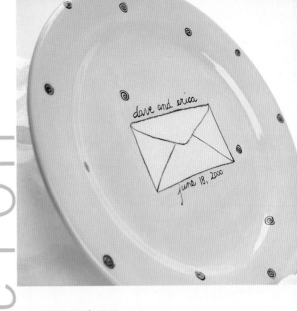

STEP 3 Paint the inside of the stamp with one solid coat of beige. Using a liner brush, paint a thin black line over the penciled border. Personalize the plate by painting images in the stamps that pertain to a special place, person, or event that you wish to commemorate. Use the other colors from the soft color palette for the images you choose. Be sure to include a postage amount in the lower right hand corner of the stamp to realistically complete the stamps. See page 249 for patterns.

VARIATION

A hand-painted commemorative plate makes the perfect wedding gift for your favorite couple. To create the design seen here, begin by mixing a small amount of white into pale yellow and paint the entire plate twice. A wide, flat brush allows for quick and even coating. Transfer the envelope pattern on page 249 to the middle of the plate. Paint the envelope with two coats of white. You should still be able to see the lines, but if not, you can re-transfer them or go over them with a pencil. Next, paint random dots using mint, lavender, and peach. Next, use a fine liner brush to add black spirals in each dot when completely dry. Then, with a pencil, hand-write the names of the couple at the top of the envelope and the wedding date under the envelope to give it the feel of a real handwritten letter. Carefully go over these with black paint. When all the paint is dry, outline the envelope with a black underglaze pencil.

PEACH   PALE YELLOW

MINT   LAVENDER

the craft painting sourcebook

dessert **PLATES**

Pastel hues and dimensional paint combine to create the iced-cake finish of this plate. Special desserts will get the attention they deserve when framed by a soothing, soft color. Since the specialty underglaze used to make the dotted pattern comes in handy squeeze bottles, perfect circles and lines are easy to achieve. Try experimenting with different bottle tops or cake decorating nibs for a variety of effects.

MATERIALS

- #3 or #4 round brush
- thin liner brush
- pencil or carbon paper
- ceramic paint underglaze colors: light pink, mint, pale yellow, peach, black, white dimensional paint

STARTING OUT

Remember always to add relief patterns last so that you don't smudge them while painting elsewhere. Practice making even-sized dots before painting them on the plate to avoid having to remove mistakes. Mistakes can be removed using a craft knife.

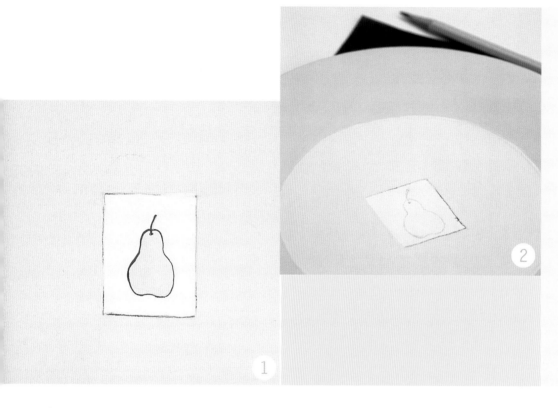

STEP 1 Draw a square or a rectangle in the center of the plate with a pencil. Draw the pear design from page 250 in the center of the rectangle.

STEP 2 Paint the inner circle of the plate with three coats of light pink, carefully avoiding the rectangle. Paint the outer circle and the underside of the plate with three coats of mint. Paint the pear with three coats of pale yellow. Let each coat dry completely before applying the next one. While the final coat of pale yellow is still damp, apply one coat of highlights with peach. When all the paint is dry, use a thin liner brush to outline the pear with one coat of black. For an impressionistic effect, try using only one or two coats of paint.

tip

Skip a step when transferring patterns by using graphite paper rather than cutting out and tracing templates. The lines will burn off in the kiln just like pencil markings.

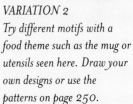
VARIATION 1

Transfer the large pear design from page 250 to the center of your dessert plate. Paint the pear with three coats of pale yellow, and paint the leaf with three coats of mint. While the final coat of pale yellow is still damp, paint the edges of the pear with peach. Paint the outer circle of the plate with three coats of peach. Use a thin liner brush to outline the pear and to add the pear's stem with one coat of black. Finally, dip the blunt end of a brush into mint paint and dab dots on the plate rim.

MINT   PALE YELLOW   PEACH

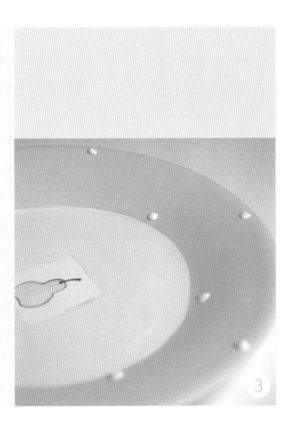

STEP 3 Squeeze a pattern of dots onto the outer circle of the plate using white dimensional paint. Here, equally spaced dots outline the inside and outside edges of the mint circle.

LIGHT PINK

MINT

PALE YELLOW

PERIWINKLE

VARIATION 2

Try different motifs with a food theme such as the mug or utensils seen here. Draw your own designs or use the patterns on page 250.

sponged
SWITCH PLATE

MATERIALS

- **household sponges**
- **ceramic paint underglaze colors: periwinkle, lavender, mint, pale yellow**

A common household element like this switch plate offers a quick and easy way to add the finishing touch to a room. A simple design utilizing soft colors will add to the ambiance while not detracting from other decorative items and furnishings. And a room with textured, faux-finished walls deserves to have a coordinated switch plate. The mottled effect of sponging serves to soften muted colors even more, enhancing the understated appeal of the classic harlequin pattern used here.

STARTING OUT
Create a custom diamond-shaped sponge for this project by tracing the switch plate on graph paper and sketching out the pattern. Once you have determined the size of the diamonds, cut a diamond out of the graph paper, utilizing this template to create a perfectly geometric, diamond-shaped sponge stamp.

STEP 1 Sponge the switch plate with one coat of periwinkle and let it dry completely. Sponge one coat of lavender, and let it dry completely.

STEP 2 Sponge diamonds across the switch plate with one coat of mint, beginning in the upper left corner. Continue with the next row, being sure to align the bottom points of the completed diamonds with the tip of the sponge.

tip
Use a brush to load the perfect amount of paint on the sponge for a clear, complete image.

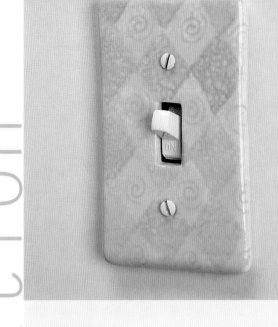

STEP 3 With a clean sponge, lightly sponge over all the diamonds with one coat of pale yellow.

VARIATION

Use a thin liner brush to paint spirals within some of the diamonds, or choose a motif from your home. This single-switch plate has a pale yellow base coat. The diamonds were sponged with beige, followed by peach. The spirals were also painted in peach.

PALE YELLOW

BEIGE

PEACH

| the craft painting sourcebook

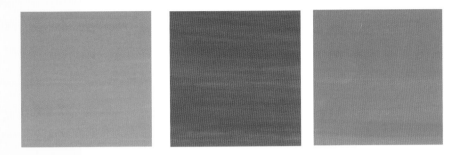

tuscan espresso
CUP & SAUCER

Earth colors are the intuitive choice for this cup and saucer, designed to serve rich, steaming espresso—of an earthy color itself. To create a truly unique set, use the same motif on each piece, but experiment with different color combinations within the earth palette. You will end up with cups and saucers that are definitely coordinated, but don't imitate each other. The professionally crisp yet fluid lines of the leaf are easy to create yourself. An easy-to-cut template on page 251 and an ordinary pencil ensure consistent results.

MATERIALS

- **#4 or #5 round brush**
- **thin liner brush**
- **pencil**
- **ceramic paint underglaze colors: tan, burnt orange, light green, black**

STARTING OUT The bottom of this cup and the inner circle of the saucer are painted the same color to visually unify the two pieces. As a final step, outlining in black where colors meet ensures a neat separation between them.

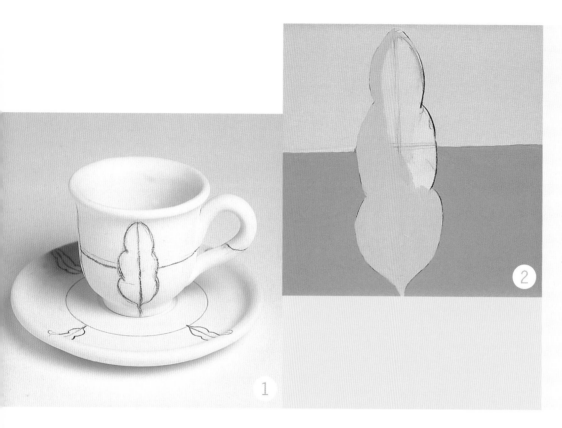

STEP 1 Pencil a circle in the center of the saucer. Then, draw a line around the circumference of the cup, dividing it into two approximately equal parts. Cut out the leaf templates on page 251. Trace the larger leaf three times randomly around the cup with a pencil. Trace the smaller leaf four times on the saucer, with each leaf opposite another. Don't worry about erasing pencil lines and smudges, as they will burn off during firing.

STEP 2 Avoiding the leaf shape outline, apply three coats of tan to the top half of the cup and the outer circle of the saucer. Apply three coats of burnt orange to the bottom half of the cup and the inner circle of the saucer. Let each coat dry completely before applying the next one. Be careful to avoid the leaf outlines. Next, paint inside the leaves with light green. For opaque leaves, use three coats; for a transparent wash, use one or two coats.

tip

To keep the color of the leaves true, be careful not to overlap the light green with any of the other colors.

tip

If you make a mistake, don't worry. When the underglaze has dried, you can scrape away the mistake with a craft knife.

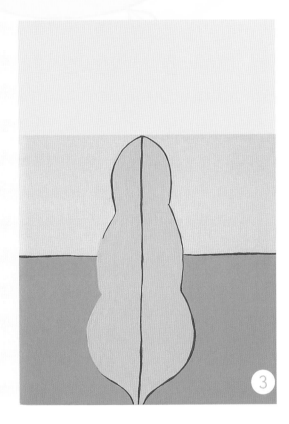

STEP 3 Outline the leaves, the inner circle on the saucer, and the line that divides the top and bottom of the cup with one coat of black using a thin liner brush. Paint a line down the middle of each leaf, sketching it in first with a pencil if desired.

variations

VARIATION 1

Use different earth tones to create a set of unique but complementary pieces. Here, brown was used in place of burnt orange.

TAN   BROWN   LIGHT GREEN

VARIATION 2

An alternate palette and improvised details can be added to complete the set.

BURNT ORANGE   TUSCAN BLUE   LIGHT GREEN

leaf & vine
SERVING PLATTER

The earthy garland framing this platter is intended to surround culinary creations, and the natural motif makes it perfect for serving homegrown food. The realistically shaded vine stands out when painted on a non-competitive but contrasting white background. The autumnal yellow and orange border enhances any dish prepared from the pick of a bountiful harvest.

MATERIALS

- **#3 or #4 round brush**
- **thin liner brush**
- **graphite paper**
- **pencil**
- **ceramic paint underglaze colors: Tuscan blue; burnt orange; deep yellow; black**

STARTING OUT To keep the scallops consistent in a freely drawn border, try sketching rough guidelines on the platter. Begin by drawing lines down the vertical and horizontal midpoints. Then divide the rest of the space like a pie.

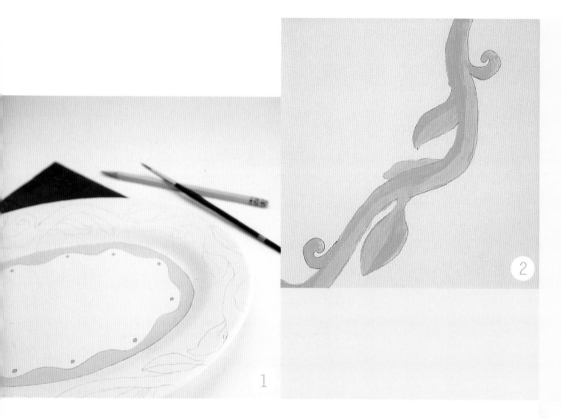

STEP 1 Using graphite paper, transfer the vine pattern on pages 254 & 255 to the outer edge of the platter. Pencil in a line around the inside of the platter, following the ridge. Draw a scalloped border freehand about 1" away from the previous pencil line. Apply three coats of deep yellow between the two lines. Let each coat dry completely before applying the next one. When the coats are completely dry, dip the handle end of your brush in burnt orange and mark a dot within each scallop of the border. Apply enough paint to make a solid, even dot.

STEP 2 Paint the vine with two coats of Tuscan blue and deep yellow, mixed in equal proportions. Before the second coat is dry, paint one coat of deep yellow highlights on one side of each leaf and on one side of the vine.

tip
For a more realistic look, paint highlights with a loose rather than a sharp, clean edge.

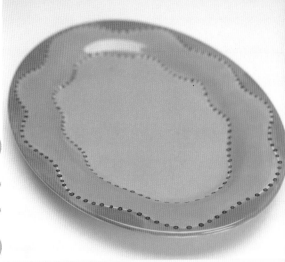

VARIATION 1

The wide scalloped border on the edge of this plat-ter dips into the bottom to create the impression that the platter, itself, is wavy. To create this pat-tern, begin by drawing a scalloped border free-hand. Using a 1" or 2" wide flat brush, paint the border with two coats of light green. Paint the inside bottom of the platter with three coats of tan. Paint the outer edge with three coats of burnt orange. When the paint is completely dry, dip the handle end of your brush in dark brown and mark dots around both wavy lines. To make smaller dots within the brown dots, dip a pencil tip in light green, or burnt orange as seen here.

TAN

LIGHT GREEN

BURNT ORANGE

BROWN

STEP 3 Using a thin liner brush, paint veins on the leaves and outline the vine, leaves, and bor-der with one coat of black.

VARIATION 2

To create the oak leaf border on this platter, transfer the pattern on page 254. Here, moss green and deep yellow leaves are set against a burnt orange background for a festive fall platter.

MOSS GREEN

BURNT ORANGE

DEEP YELLOW

painting glass

Painting Glass is a guide to creating colorful designs and patterns on glass surfaces by using color shaping techniques. Capture the luminosity and translucency of colored glass in just a few simple steps. Learn how to achieve unique transparent effects simulating molded and blown glass.

This section is designed to introduce you to an innovative approach to decorative painting on glass. You will become acquainted with the Color Shapers through basic exercises on glass sheets and 12 projects with easy-to-follow, step-by-step instructions, as well as pattern variations for each project. The projects draw inspiration from historical sources and interpret the characteristics of art glass in terms of color, design and pattern from ancient times to the present. The styles represented include ancient glass from the Mediterranean region, Islamic golden lustre glass, Venetian, Millefiori, Art Nouveau, Art Deco, and contemporary blown glass.

The glass objects for the projects presented are readily available in home goods stores, craft stores, and second-hand shops. Color Shaper sizes can be substituted if you do not have the size specified in the materials list. Combine imagination with color shaping, and discover a new and exciting alternative to decorative painting.

PALETTE   Use the suggested palette or try mixing new color combinations.

CUTTING TEMPLATE   Diagrams show how to notch the color shaper tools to attain the desired effect.

PATTERN SKETCHES   A drawing is a helpful guide for the final piece.

STEP-BY-STEP INSTRUCTIONS
The final patterns are achieved by following the steps.

basics

The patterns and designs featured on the glass projects in this book are created using the Color Shaper, an exciting new painting tool manufactured by Royal Sovereign, Ltd. Color shaping is a creative solution to traditional painting.

Color Shapers are rubber-tipped tools that come in a variety of sizes and shapes. The large Color Shapers speed up the decorative painting process by patterning large areas in a single stroke, while fine detail can be achieved with the smaller sizes. The concept behind color shaping is subtracting wet paint from the glass surface and leaving behind lines, marks and strokes. Combine simple strokes to create beautiful designs and unique effects. The Color Shaper's gray tip offers good control in wet paint. Clean the tip after use by dipping into soapy water or alcohol and wiping dry. In the projects that follow, you will discover the amazing effects of color shaping on glass, and with a little practice you will achieve polished results.

basic materials

Here is a list and description of some of the basic materials you will need to create the projects that follow.

prepared surface	Degrease the glass surface with soapy water or alcohol.
Color Shapers	Rubber-tipped tools in various sizes and shapes that are used to carve images in wet paint.
brushes	In addition to Color Shapers, the projects use the following paint brushes: 1" (3 cm) soft wash brush, #12 flat shader brush, #1 and #4 script liners, and #8 round brush. Mixtique brushes by Loew-Cornelle are recommended, as they are designed specifically for glass painting; the natural bristles apply paint evenly, leaving behind no brushmarks. If these are not available at your local art and craft store, look for soft bristle brushes instead.
glass paint	The projects in this book use Pēbēo glass paints, Vitrea 160, transparent water-based paints for glass. The white and metallic gold paint used on projects in this book are from Pēbēo's Porcelain 150 collection, due to their opacity. Other transparent glass paints are available on the market. Carefully read the manufacturer's instructions.
extender	A drop (literally) of water mixed with glass paints will extend the open time, that is, the time in which the paint is wet and can be worked. To produce the color shaping effects, the paint must remain wet long enough to subtract the color.

baking guide

Color shaping involves a layering process. Each step must be protected before proceeding with the next layer. Follow these guidelines to ensure maximum results:

dry

Although the manufacturer's instructions say it is necessary for the paint to dry 24 hours before baking, or bubbling will occur, here is an alternative approach for speeding up the drying process: Place project in a cool oven, set at 150 degrees F (60C) for ten minutes. Turn the oven off, let the object cool and remove it from oven. This step simply dries the wet paint. This is an ideal temperature for drying because bubbling will not occur. (If you need to dry a painted stripe or brushstroke, you can simply use a hair dryer to blow it dry.)

dry and set

This step combines drying wet paint and heat setting for a tough finish before applying another layer of paint. Place project in a 150-degree F (60C) oven for ten minutes to dry. Increase the temperature to 325 degrees F (160C) and bake for 20 minutes. Turn oven off, cool down gradually and remove the object from oven. This process produces a sealed paint finish that is necessary before applying another layer of color.

final baking

Place completed project in cool oven and set at 150 degrees F (60C) for 10 minutes to dry the final layer of paint. Increase the temperature to 325 degrees F (160C) and bake for 30 minutes. Turn the oven off, cool down gradually and remove from oven. This final step produces a permanent paint finish and a functional surface.

beads and findings

Embellish painted glass with beads and findings. Colored glass beads and jewelry findings can enhance and add character to a painted glass object. In many instances, such embellishments can produce the finishing touch. Experiment by combining several types of beads to trim or accent your project.

Bead stores and crafts suppliers offer many different kinds of beads in a variety of sizes, shapes and colors. Ideally, a flat-backed bead is best suited for adhering to a glass surface. Use a glue or cement made for glass for the strongest adherence.

glowing window ornament

MATERIALS

Glass window ornament

3" (77 mm) Curve Wide Color Shaper, cut and notched (see diagram)

1" (3 cm) soft wash brush

The beauty of colored glass is best revealed through filtered sunlight. A simple glass window ornament exposes glowing colors through illumination. This first project takes a triangular glass ornament and repeats a multicolored scalloped pattern. Turquoise, green, and yellow combine with translucent magenta to catch the sun, mirroring the multicolored glass rods used in contemporary blown glass. Add curves and spirals to create intricate patterns. Design several glowing ornaments of various shapes and sizes, then string them together to hang from a sunny window.

glass paint: yellow, green, turquoise, and magenta

The 3" (77 mm) Curve Wide Color Shaper, cut and notched, creates the striped scallop pattern in a single stroke. If using a narrower width Color Shaper, you may have to repeat the step to finish the pattern. To vary your design, use the #6 Flat Chisel Color Shaper to form spiral shapes.

A simple line drawing on paper will help you to plan your design. Play with repetitive lines, scallops, and curves to form your pattern.

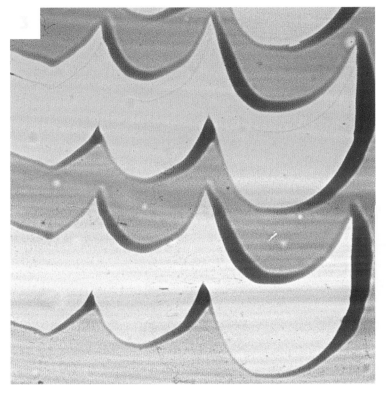

Try to apply the paint evenly with a light brush stroke to prevent ridged lines.

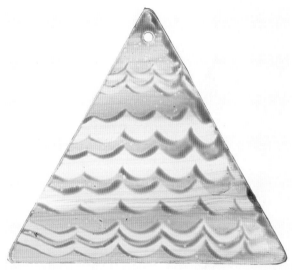

step one With the soft wash brush, make three stripes, in yellow, green, and turquoise to cover the entire background. Dry and set (see p. 77).

step two With a wash brush, apply a layer of magenta paint over prepared background.

step three Cut and notch the 3" (77 mm) Curve Wide Color Shaper (see diagram). Using the cut and notched Color Shaper, form a scalloped pattern in a single stroke. The size of the project makes it very easy to handle the technique. Follow final baking instructions in the basic materials section (see p. 77).

stylish striped frame

MATERIALS

Glass frame

1-1/2" (38 mm) Curve Wide Color Shaper, cut and notched (see diagram)

#6 Flat Chisel Color Shaper

1" (3 cm) soft wash brush

Glass marker: turquoise (or you may use turquoise paint with a liner brush)

Flat glass beads for embellishing (optional)

Transform a simple square of glass into an objet d'art through color and pattern. The interplay of citrus yellow with fuchsia combined with linear patterns leads to interesting results. Contemporary blown glass is the reference point for this project, borrowing inspiration from layers of transparent colors as seen in today's art glass. Choose a frame with a smooth glass border. To create your own, rest two pieces of glass, cut to size, on a plate stand or small easel. Paint and color shape the border, insert your photo, and display your personalized piece of art on a mantle or shelf.

glass paint: lemon yellow, fuchsia, turquoise

▷ To produce clean intersecting lines of color, use the 1-1/2" (38 mm) Curve Wide Color Shaper, cut and notched. The #6 Flat Chisel Color Shaper allows you to paint lines, stripes, and zigzags for visual interest.

Plan the width of the border for the frame on a sheet of paper. Create a simple layout based on the measurements of the glass to secure your design concept. Vary the placement of the intersecting lines to enhance your pattern.

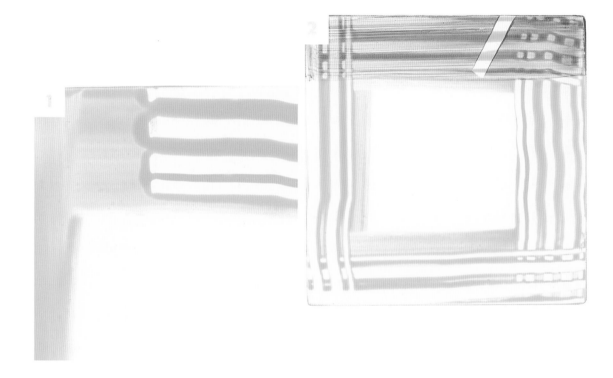

step one   Using the 1 " (3 cm) wash brush, apply yellow paint (thinned with a drop of water) to the border areas of the frame. Apply paint to all four sides at the same time, to create intersecting lines in the four corners. Using the 1-1/2" Curve Wide Color Shaper, cut and notched, form stripes through the wet glaze on all four sides using firm pressure. Wipe the shaper as you go along. Notice the interesting patterns in the four corners where the lines intersect. Dry and set (see p. 77).

step two   Apply the fuchsia paint (thinned with a drop of water) over the yellow layer. (You may do this step in sections, one side at a time.) Using the #6 Flat Chisel Color Shaper, form a series of lines through the wet paint, using firm pressure. Alternate directions to form a pattern. Notice the color changes as burnt orange becomes part of the palette.

step three Using the turquoise glass pen or turquoise paint with a liner brush, make a squiggly line, forming a square within the frame. Follow final baking instructions.

optional step Embellish the finished frame with beads.

tip

Color coordinate your painted frame to enhance your favorite photo.

striking storage container

Combine beauty with utility in a series of painted glass storage containers. The combed linear pattern is an interpretation of ancient core-formed glass from the Mediterranean region. Spirals and intricate linear designs mirror the spirals of molten glass from this period. Turquoise, blue, and yellow reflect the colors typically used. Choose a box from a variety of heights and widths, then fill one with cotton puffs to accent your bathroom.

MATERIALS

Glass storage container

3" (77 mm) Curve Wide Color Shaper, cut and notched (see diagram) (You may substitute any of the other Wide Curve Color Shapers.)

1" (3 cm) soft wash brush

glass paint: turquoise

◁ The 3" (77 mm) Curve Wide Color Shaper cleanly removes the paint in one step. When you cut and notch the Color Shaper, clear stripes form wavy, zigzag, or combed patterns.

A quick sketch on paper will help you plan the direction of the combing and will solidify your design concept. Explore the width of the stripes, from narrow to broad. Customize the notched tip of your Color Shaper to reflect your design.

step one With the 1" (3 cm) wash brush, apply turquoise paint, thinned with water, to the cover of the box. Using the 3" (77 mm) cut and notched Curve Wide Color Shaper, make wavy stripes through the wet glaze, applying firm pressure. If you use a narrow Shaper, you will have to repeat the step to cover the entire area.

Test the color shaping technique on a sheet of palette paper or a scrap piece of glass.

step two Continue applying paint and color shaping each side of the box, a section at a time. Follow final baking instructions.

elegant perfume bottle

MATERIALS

Glass perfume bottle

1-1/2" (38 mm) Curve Wide Color Shaper, cut and notched (see diagram) (other sizes may be substituted)

#6 Cup Round Color Shaper

1" (3 cm) soft wash brush

#4 script liner brush

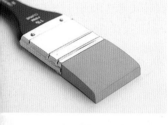

The perfume bottle translates the characteristics of contemporary Venetian glass. The role of color is emphasized and careful consideration is given to tint, composition and depth. The project combines translucent color with opaque areas. Notice the interplay of light through the striped blue areas. The design can be easily adapted to fit other bottle shapes. For instance, if the stopper is smaller, you might try incorporating the black and white pattern somewhere on the bottle itself.

glass paint: azure blue, deep blue-violet, black, white, and gold

▷ Vertical and diagonal lines are clearly defined with the 1-1/2" (38 mm) Curve Wide Color Shaper, cut and notched for a series of stripes. Use the #6 Cup Round Color Shaper to create rounded petal strokes.

Sketch the bottle on paper to assess its shape. Organize the design elements to fit the form of the bottle. Vary the pattern by changing the width of the stripes, from a delicate to a bold pattern.

step one Apply a thin coat of azure blue, thinned with a drop of water, over the entire bottle. Dry and set (see p. 77).

step two Using a 1" (3 cm) wash brush, apply the deep blue-violet paint, thinned with a drop of water, over the prepared basecoat in sections. Pull the 1-1/2" (38 mm) Curve Wide Color Shaper, cut and notched, through the wet paint, using firm pressure, to make stripes.

step three Apply an even coat of white paint over the entire stopper, using the 1" (3 cm) wash brush. Dry and set.

tip

When creating the petal stroke with the Cup Round Color Shaper, push down and away into the wet paint using firm pressure. Keep the pressure at the tip of the Shaper.

4

3

step four Using the 1" (3 cm) wash brush, apply black paint, thinned with a drop of water, over the cooled white paint in sections. With the #6 Cup Round Color Shaper, form short petal strokes by pushing away through the wet paint. Accent with gold using the # 4 script liner brush. Follow final baking instructions.

colorful wine decanter

A beautifully painted decanter can serve as a showpiece on your table. Use the decanter to serve wine or ice water to dinner-party guests. The interaction of vibrant colors and latticework recalls the 19th century art of interweaving multi-colored glass rods. Yellow, white, and turquoise form the underlayer of color, while magenta twists are color shaped to create a lattice effect.

MATERIALS

Glass wine decanter

#6 Flat Chisel Color Shaper

1" (3 cm) soft wash brush

#4 script liner brush

#8 round brush

#12 flat shader

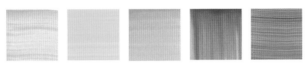

glass paints: white, yellow, magenta, and turquoise

◁ The #6 Flat Chisel Color Shaper helps you to easily create the twisted lattice pattern, forming twists and squiggle lines through the paint. Use the 3" (77 mm) Curve Wide Color Shaper, cut and notched, to vary your design with diagonal lines.

starting out

Plan your design on a sketch of the decanter to see how the edges will come together. Play with the width of the stripes using brushes of various sizes.

step one   Using the wash brush, paint vertical stripes in white on all four sides. Dry with a hair dryer. With the #12 flat shader brush, paint a series of horizontal stripes in light yellow (yellow mixed with white) over the white on all four sides. Blow dry.

step two With the #4 script liner, form a series of narrow vertical stripes in light turquoise (turquoise mixed with white). Dry and set (see p. 77).

step three With the wash brush, apply an even layer of magenta over the plaid background. Using the #6 Flat Chisel Color Shaper, form a series of diagonal twists first in one direction, then immediately in the opposite direction. Accent top portion and stopper in yellow and magenta, adding a few petal strokes around the stopper. Follow final baking instructions.

Practice twisted lattice strokes on palette paper or glass sheet first. Simply move the #6 Flat Chisel Color Shaper back and forth in the wet paint to form a squiggle line.

iridescent candle holder

MATERIALS

Glass candle holder

3" (77 mm) Curve Wide Color Shaper, cut and notched (see template)

1" (3 cm) soft wash brush

#4 script liner brush

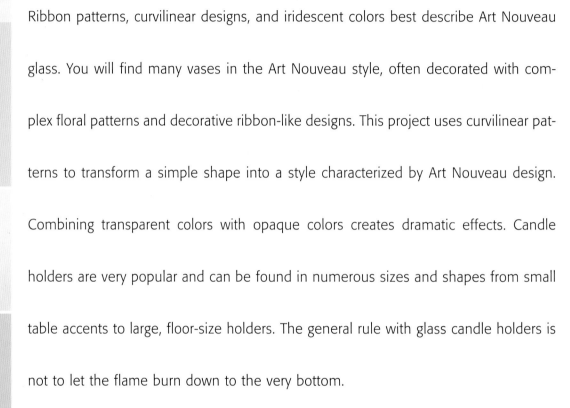

Ribbon patterns, curvilinear designs, and iridescent colors best describe Art Nouveau glass. You will find many vases in the Art Nouveau style, often decorated with complex floral patterns and decorative ribbon-like designs. This project uses curvilinear patterns to transform a simple shape into a style characterized by Art Nouveau design.

Combining transparent colors with opaque colors creates dramatic effects. Candle holders are very popular and can be found in numerous sizes and shapes from small table accents to large, floor-size holders. The general rule with glass candle holders is not to let the flame burn down to the very bottom.

glass paints: violet, blue-violet, white, and gold

The 3" (77 mm) Curve Wide Color Shaper, cut and notched, forms a series of broad repetitive lines in a single stroke. Vary your strokes to create a scalloped or ribbon pattern.

A scale drawing of your candle holder will help you identify the best areas to color shape. You will get a better sense of design possibilities by plotting your ideas on paper. Draw repeated lines in a curvilinear direction to form a pattern.

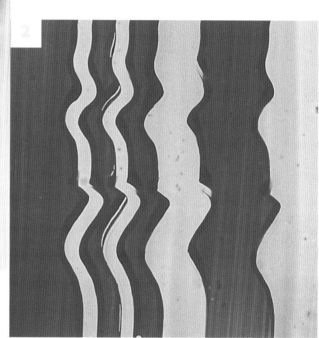

step one   With the wash brush, apply an even layer of transparent violet paint over the entire surface. Dry and set (see p. 77).

step two   Apply a layer of light blue-violet paint (blue-violet mixed with white) evenly over the entire surface. Thin the paint with a single drop of water. Using the 3" (77 mm) Curve Wide Color Shaper, cut and notched, form a wavy line through the wet paint. Try to match the lines as you come to the end. You can stop half way, wipe the tip and get a better grip for the second half of the project. Dry and set.

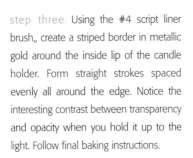

tip

Keep the paint wet long enough to complete the stripe.

step three Using the #4 script liner brush,, create a striped border in metallic gold around the inside lip of the candle holder. Form straight strokes spaced evenly all around the edge. Notice the interesting contrast between transparency and opacity when you hold it up to the light. Follow final baking instructions.

lustrous candy dish

MATERIALS

Glass candy dish

#6 Angle Chisel Color
Shaper

1" (3 cm) soft wash brush

#4 script liner brush

#10 flat brush

The golden hue of this candy dish has its origins in the ancient tradition of Islamic craftsmen, who applied a metallic powder to glass and ceramics, creating lustre glass. This project interprets the qualities of golden lustre with luminous effects. Using a wash to recreate the translucent golden glow, a series of ferns is then color shaped onto the dish. A sugar bowl can be substituted for a candy dish.

glass paint: white, turquoise, and gold

▶ Form a series of ferns using the angled edge of the #6 Angle Chisel Color Shaper. The long, sharp edge is ideal for broad or tapered leaf strokes.

Begin with a sketch. Organize a couple of simple leaf designs on paper to form a repetitive pattern. A layout will help arrange the spacing. A single leaf can be repeated, or combine a cluster of leaves to form a design.

step one Using the wash brush, apply a thin layer of turquoise paint over the entire candy dish, cover and bottom. You will achieve a transparent effect. Dry and set (see p. 77).

step two Mix white and turquoise to form a light turquoise. Using the #10 flat brush, combine three s-strokes to create a leaf motif. Repeat this step to complete the border pattern around both pieces of glass. Dry and set.

Practice the s-stroke with the #10 flat brush on a sheet of palette paper. Load the brush evenly on both sides to produce a nice clean stroke.

step three Using the wash brush, apply a layer of gold paint over candy dish. With the #6 Angle Chisel Color Shaper, form a series of ferns through the wet paint. Use the angled edge of the shaper and push away forming a stroke mark. Clean the tip as you go along. Repeat this step on the cover.

step four Using the #4 script liner brush, paint metallic gold stripes around the bottom of the bowl. Follow final baking instructions.

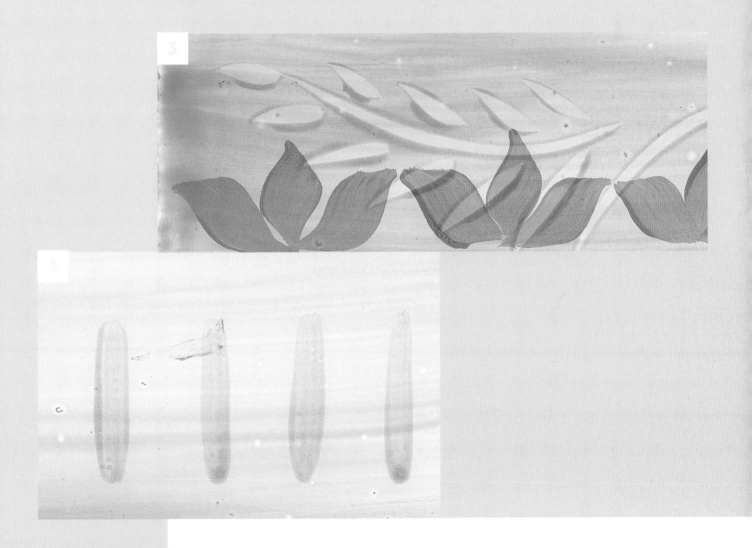

dramatic pouring pitcher

Place this beautifully painted pitcher on a bright shelf or tabletop to display the luminous plaid of red and yellow. Hints of pink and orange are revealed as light shines through the glass. The intersecting diagonal lines of this design are interpreted from a 20th century Italian glass-making technique, Scozzese, or "Scottish," for its tartan-like qualities. The glass process involved criss-crossing inlaid rods of different colored glass. Use the color shaping techniques to create this effect with paint.

glass paint: yellow, white, and red.

MATERIALS

Glass pitcher

1-1/2" (38 mm) Curve Wide Color Shaper, cut and notched (see diagram) (This pattern uses two different cut and notched tips for a varied effect; however, you can work with the same tip if you wish.)

1" (3 cm) wash brush

a

b

◀ Apply firm pressure to the 1-1/2" (38 mm) Curve Wide Color Shaper, cut and notched, to achieve clean, diagonal lines. Use two different cut and notched tips to create intersecting lines of various dimensions. To vary your design, use the 3" (77 mm) Curve Wide Color Shaper, cut and notched, to form a wider criss-cross of lines.

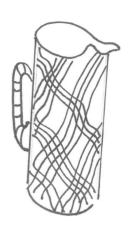

Plan the direction of the lines and form the plaid first in the form of a sketch. To

vary the width of the plaid, customize your cut and notched Curve Wide

Color Shaper to reflect your design.

step one With the wash brush, apply a layer of light yellow (yellow mixed with white, and thinned with a drop of water) glass paint over the entire pitcher. This application needs to be done in one step. Using the 1-1/2" (38 mm) Curve Wide Color Shaper, cut and notched, make a series of diagonal lines in one direction through the wet paint. Use firm pressure when color shaping to achieve nice clean lines. Cover the entire pitcher with a lined pattern. Dry and set (see p. 77).

step two With the wash brush, apply a layer of red paint, thinned with a drop of water, over the entire yellow striped background.

step three Using the 1-1/2" (38 mm) Curve Wide Color Shaper, cut and notched, make a series of diagonal lines in the opposite direction. Use the second cut and notched tip here to vary the effect. Follow final baking instructions.

Find a comfortable way to hold the pitcher so that you can create continuous, clean lines.

semi-abstract vase

MATERIALS

Glass vase

#6 Angle Chisel Color
Shaper (other sizes may
be substituted)

#10 Cup Round Color
Shaper (other sizes may
be substituted)

1" (3 cm) soft wash brush

#4 script liner brush

#12 flat brush

The interaction of color and pattern characterizes Art Deco, where semi-abstract design elements are drawn from natural plant forms such as leaves, flowers, fruits, berries, etc. The palette of vibrant yellow and turquoise is inspired by the rich colors of Art Deco design. New colors emerge as the colors overlap. The pattern featured here uses a semi-abstract flower to form the overall pattern. A few simple brush-strokes create the flower shape. Brushstrokes combined with color shaping techniques result in a complex pattern.

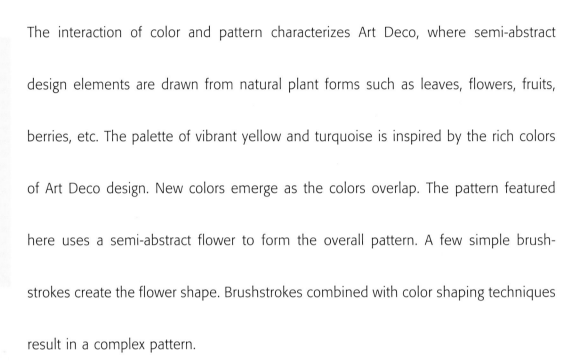

glass paint: white, yellow, and turquoise

Forming long and short rounded strokes, the #10 Cup Round Color Shaper creates perfect petal shapes. Use the long, sharp edge of the #6 Angle Chisel Color Shaper to pattern a zigzag line. To vary your design, use the 1-1/2" (38 mm) Curve Wide Color Shaper, cut and notched, to achieve a clear, scalloped flower.

Collect some ideas

by researching Art Deco designs. There are many books on the subject with wonderful colored

patterns. Experiment with one or two simple design elements and apply them to a scaled

drawing of your project. Consider placement and spacing. This pattern uses basic strokes to

form the underlying design.

step one A repetitive design made up of basic strokes is the underlying pattern for this project. Simple strokes such as a c-stroke and comma strokes are combined to form the repeating motif. Use your imagination and combine strokes to form a design. For this project, make a c-stroke in white with the 1" (3 cm) wash brush to form the heart of the design. Form comma strokes with the #12 flat brush, and short strokes with the #4 script liner. Dry and set (see p. 77).

step two Using the 1" (3 cm) wash brush and #12 flat brush, create additional c-strokes and s-strokes in yellow, spilling on to the previous white strokes. Dry and set.

These steps are easy to do because you can do them in sections, completing the pattern as you go along.

step three A Using the 1" (3 cm) wash brush, create a c-stroke in turquoise over the base c-stroke. With the #10 Cup Round Color Shaper, form petals through the wet paint, pushing away. Notice the interesting effects where the yellow and white show through.

step three B Create s-strokes in turquoise with the 1" (3 cm) wash brush, overlaying the previous comma strokes. With the #6 Angle Chisel Color Shaper, form a zigzag line through the wet paint. Follow final baking instructions.

vibrant sunflower pattern bowl

A shallow glass bowl is an ideal way to display favorite collections, such as seashells or sea glass. Or color it with vivid paints and display in a sunny window. This glass bowl is painted with luminous colors inspired by the vibrant hues of contemporary blown glass. A semi-abstract floral design is repeated to create an overall pattern. Half-circle shapes form the underlayer of the flower. For this project, choose a glass bowl that has a flat brimmed edge to work well as a border area. Use it to hold wrapped candy or the day's mail. Contact with food is not recommended.

MATERIALS

Glass bowl

#6 Flat Chisel Color Shaper

1" (25 mm) soft wash brush

#4 script liner brush

#8 round brush

Flat glass beads

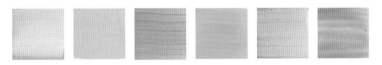

glass paints: white, yellow, turquoise, orange, blue-violet, and red

◀ The #6 Flat Chisel Color Shaper creates simple short and long lines and squiggles. Applying the Color Shaper back and forth over the sunflower petals melds colors together and creates new ones.

Create a design layout on paper first. Draw a large circle, representing the bowl. Repeat a series of small semi-circles to form the border and inside section. To give an idea of placement and spacing, add squiggles over the semi-circles, suggesting the color shaping technique.

step one Create the underpainting that consists of base semi-circles in yellow outlined in turquoise. Mix white and yellow paint together to make a light yellow. Load the 1" (25 mm) wash brush with yellow paint and form a series of half circles to create the border and inside section. Next, mix white and turquoise together. With the #4 script liner brush, outline each of the circles using a single stroke of the brush. Dry and set (see p. 77).

step two Using the #8 round brush, paint petal strokes in orange over each of the semi-circles and in blue-violet between the circles. Practice the strokes on paper first to get an idea of the amount of pressure on the brush. This completes the underpainting step. Dry and set.

step three Using the wash brush, apply transparent pink paint (red mixed with white), thinned with a single drop of water, over the prepared background in sections. With the #6 Flat Chisel Color Shaper, make zigzags in the wet glaze over each of the circles. Using firm pressure, move the Color Shaper back and forth, subtracting the wet glaze. Clean the tip as you go along. You may wish to practice this step on a piece of scrap glass first. Notice the interesting color changes that occur. Continue this process until the entire bowl is color shaped.

step four Compete the pattern by painting small petal strokes in gold using the #4 script liner brush. Follow final baking instructions.

tip Practice making the half-circle stroke. A clean sweep of the brush will give a quality stroke with no ridges.

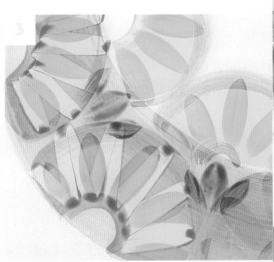

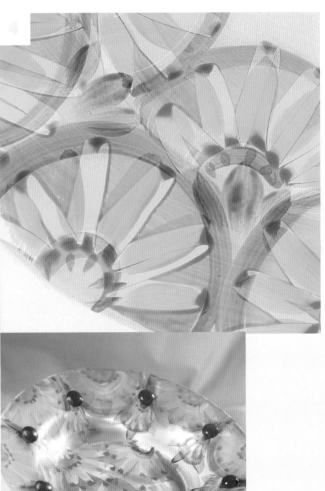

exotic cake dome

MATERIALS

Glass cake dome with pedestal

#6 Angle Chisel Color Shaper

1" (3 cm) wash brush

#12 flat shader brush

#4 script liner brush

#1 script liner brush

Create a unique yet familiar pattern as you rely on the shapes of nature for inspiration. The repeating leaf design produces a colorful, abstract motif, representative of the Art Deco period. Choose an unusual leaf or seashell to create your design. Repeat the shape to form a decorative pattern. A leaf design is repeated here to form a border around the dome as well as on the pedestal base. Portions of the dome are left clear to reveal that special dessert stored within. You can substitute a cheese dome for a smaller project.

glass paints: white, turquoise, yellow, and magenta

▷ Use the long, sharp edge of the #6 Angle Chisel Color Shaper to run zigzag lines over each leaf design. Use other Colors Shapers to vary your art; the #6 Cup Round forms rounded strokes and petal shapes, and the 3" (77 mm) Curve Wide, cut and notched, cleanly forms wavy stripes.

Select a single design

element (this project features a leaf but you can experiment with other motifs) and repea

it to form a pattern. Prepare a simple sketch to secure your concept. Try varying the

size of your leaf or other design element for even more visual interest.

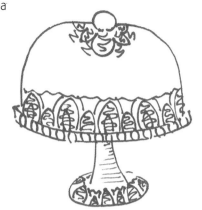

step one A Use the 1" (3 cm) wash brush and the #12 flat shader brush to create an alternating leaf pattern in white by varying the sizes of the leaves. Form leaf strokes around the sides of the dome and at the base of the pedestal.

step one B Using the #12 flat shader brush, overlay small leaf strokes on top of the white using a light turquoise (turquoise mixed with white). Outline each leaf using the #4 script liner brush (or a 1" script liner). Dry and set (see p. 77).

step two With the wash brush, apply yellow paint over the prepared pattern. Using the #6 Angle Chisel Color Shaper, form a zigzag line through the wet paint on each leaf. Use the #1 script liner brush to edge the border with a squiggly line. This completes the bottom portion of the dome and pedestal.

step three With the wash brush, paint a series of scalloped strokes in white around the top of the dome. Add an s-stroke between each scallop using the #12 flat shader brush.

step four A With the #4 script liner brush, paint a series of linear leaf strokes in light turquoise. Dry and set.

step four B With the wash brush, apply a yellow band over the prepared background. Using the #6 Angle Chisel Color Shaper, make a series of zigzags through the wet paint. At this time, accent the very top portion of dome, lip, and pedestal in magenta. Follow final baking instructions.

tip
You can apply the yellow paint layer and color shape this pattern in sections.

millefiori bowl

MATERIALS

Deep glass bowl

1-1/2" (38 mm) Curve Wide Color Shaper, cut and notched (see diagram)

#6 Flat Chisel Color Shaper

1" (3 cm) soft wash brush

In traditional millefiori, canes of glass are sliced to create a mosaiclike effect. This technique dates back to Roman times and is used in Venetian glass. The definition of millefiori is a "thousand flowers" because many of the small circular shapes form intricate floral designs. Contemporary art glass uses this traditional technique to create abstract designs. The painted bowl is a contemporary interpretation of millefiori where simple circular shapes are repeated to form a pattern. Only the outside of the bowl is decorated, making it safe to store fruit, nuts, or candy inside.

glass paints: white, blue, citrus yellow (yellow mixed with white and a drop of green), turquoise, and magenta

▶ Wet paint is cleanly subtracted using the 1-1/2" (38 mm) Curve Wide Color Shaper, and the cut and notched tip forms clear stripes. The #6 Flat Chisel creates curvilinear and doughnut shapes. To vary your design, use the 3" (77 mm) Curve Wide, cut and notched, forming tight waves and looped lines. The #6 Cup Round can be used to create petal strokes.

Sketch your design on paper first to plan out the circles, lines, and shapes. A random, tossed pattern works well for this design. Try grouping sets of circles with some overlap.

step one   With a 1" (3 cm) wash brush, paint broad vertical stripes in white around the outside of the bowl. Dry and set (see p. 77).

step two A With a wash brush, paint broad vertical stripes over prepared background in light blue (blue mixed with white), spaced out evenly. Using the 1-1/2" (38 mm) Curve Wide Color Shaper, cut and notched, form a vertical zigzag pattern through the wet paint. Dry and set.

step two B With the wash brush, paint vertical stripes in yellow over prepared background. Using the 1-1/2" (38 mm) Curve Wide Color Shaper, cut and notched, make a horizontal striped pattern. Dry and set.

step three With the wash brush, apply magenta paint over the prepared background in sections. Using the #6 Flat Chisel Color Shaper, make doughnut shapes through the wet paint, representing canes of glass. Cover entire bowl with a random selection of doughnut shapes. Dry and set.

step four With a wash brush, apply a layer of turquoise paint over patterned background in sections. Using the #6 Flat Chisel Color Shaper, form additional doughnut shapes through the wet paint. The overlay of colors and shapes results in an intricate design. The play of light, color, and transparency contributes to unusual effects. Follow final baking instructions.

tip Use firm pressure when forming the doughnut shapes; wipe the tip of your shaper as you go along.

painting furniture

BASICS OF
painting *furniture*

Painting is a great way to breathe new life into an old piece of furniture—or even to transform an ordinary newer piece of furniture into a focal point of a room. You may find an old end table in the attic or a piano bench at a yard sale. When you look at it, you're drawn to it, though you don't quite know why. You can see that even in a state of utter disrepair, the piece has an inherent charm. But how can you bring that out? This book provides several pattern and finish ideas that will inspire you to unlock the potential of any piece of furniture, from chairs to bureaus to tables to cabinets and more.

What you decide to paint is as important as how you decide to paint it. Obviously, a larger piece of furniture is going to make a stronger statement in a room than a smaller piece. Keep this in mind when you plan the piece. An elaborate and vibrant design painted on a large armoire is going to draw more attention than the same design on a small ladder-back chair. And conversely, a subtle stenciled pattern painted on a small, wall-mounted shelf may get lost, while the same pattern painted as a border treatment around the top of a dining room table will not.

As you begin, notice that each project is rated for level of difficulty:

a single paintbrush indicates no experience needed

two paintbrushes indicate easy projects

three paintbrushes indicate more challenging projects

four paintbrushes indicate projects to tackle once you have some experience

The Essentials

Before you begin any painted furniture project, make sure you are prepared. There's nothing worse than having to stop a project in the middle to run out and get the right size brush or the furniture wax you need to do an aging technique. Here are some basic materials that are always good to have on hand:
- Several sharpened number-two pencils
- White chalk
- Tracing paper
- Sheets of oak tag or thin cardboard
- Smudge-resistant carbon paper
- Screwdriver to remove furniture hardware
- Sandpaper ranging from extra-fine to medium grit
- Painter and artist brushes in various sizes
- Exacto knife and spare blades
- Ruler and/or T-square
- Drop cloths
- Several clean cotton rags
- Empty jars of various sizes—including film canisters—for storing portions of paint mixtures you've created plus containers such as coffee cans for mixing paint
- Stirring sticks for mixing colors
- Painter's masking tape of varying widths

BASICS OF painting

Surfaces

More often than not, when you embark on a painted furniture project, you'll be working on wood. However, you may have an old metal cabinet that needs a facelift. Perhaps you bought a dresser in particleboard that you'd like to cheer up, or you'd rather paint over than replace the Formica in your kitchen. While it is possible to work with these surfaces—which we did in one example on page 163, the Seventies Chic cabinet—wood is by far the easiest surface to work with and is the surface we will be focusing on here.

Preparation

In this book, and especially in the patterns section, we focus on a particular section of the whole piece—a door, a drawer, a panel. But when you paint a piece of furniture, you have to deal with the piece as a whole.

Before you begin any painted furniture project, take a close look at the piece you will be painting. Are there any splits, knots, cracks, or missing chunks of wood that need to be filled? Also, if it is an old piece, is it stable?

Do any parts—like a chair leg—need to be replaced before you get started? You don't want to put in the painting time, only to have the piece fall apart on you when someone sits in it.

Does the piece have handles, knobs, pulls, or hinges? If so, remove these before getting started. It's easier to sand, clean, and paint the surface when hardware is already removed—even if you are planning to paint them in the same way as the piece. This will allow you to get a more even coverage on both the furniture and the hardware.

Does the piece have glass doors or partial glass doors? If so, remove them. Or, protect the glass from paint by masking off the perimeter of the glass with 1-inch (3 cm) masking tape. While you can always scrape off any paint you get on the glass with a razor blade later, peeling off masking tape is an easier, more time-effective method. Once you've addressed these issues, you can begin the process of getting your piece ready to paint.

furniture

When the piece is ready, place it on a drop cloth. You can use the plastic type available in any hardware store, or try an old sheet—at least for the sanding phase. When you're done with sanding, you'll be grateful to wrap the residue up and throw it away—and not break out the vacuum. Whatever material you are working with, the sanding phase is an integral part of the process. For all types of wood, you'll want to use a medium to fine-grit sandpaper—150 grit is best—to get the piece smooth and ready for painting. Too coarse a grit will score the surface, while too fine a grit will not achieve the required smoothness. You can sand the piece by hand, or use an electric sander, which will save a lot of time.

After you've completely sanded the piece, run your hand along it, looking for bumps and splinters. When you're satisfied with the smoothness of the surface, wipe away residue with a damp cloth or a tack cloth. Once this phase is completed, remove the drop cloth you used for sanding and replace it with a clean one for painting. While some projects don't require a piece to be primed before you begin painting, most will benefit from at least one coat of primer. For the projects in this book,

we used a water-based primer. A water-based primer is not only easier to clean from brushes, it also dries faster. Paint the entire piece of furniture with primer and allow each coat of primer to dry for at least two hours. Once the primer is dry, proceed with the base coat. Then follow the directions for the project you have chosen.

Brushes

You should have a variety of brushes of different sizes, thicknesses, shapes, and materials on hand before beginning a painted furniture project.

Sponge brushes are great for high-coverage projects—for painting primer and base coats. Depending on what you are painting, a 2- to 3-inch (5 to 8 cm) sponge brush will probably do the trick. The best part about sponge brushes is that they are inexpensive and disposable—no clean-up needed. Also, for projects that require a very smooth surface, you don't have to worry about bristle marks—or stray bristles. They create smooth, even strokes.

Wide-bristle brushes (2- to 3-inch [5 to 8 cm]) are also good for large coverage projects, like painting the primer and base coats. The coverage you get from a bristle brush is basically the same as with sponge brush, but less smooth. Rule of thumb: quality counts when using these types of brushes. When properly cleaned, you can hold on to a high-quality brush forever. A low-quality brush will fall apart after a few uses.

Smaller sponge or bristle brushes (1-inch [3 cm]) are great for touch ups. It's always good to have a few of these on hand. Art brushes are essential for detail work, intricate patterns, and small areas. These come in all different sizes, shapes, and densities. Round brushes are best for filling in templates, while flat brushes work great for painting areas between masking tape. Use a liner brush for thin borders, outlines, and details.

Paint

For most of the projects in this book, we either used latex-based household interior paint or acrylic art paint.

The household interior paint works perfectly for base coats, finishes, and many of the patterns. Unless the project calls for you to use a flat, satin, or high-gloss paint, the finish you use can be determined by your own personal preference. The best thing about using household paint is that you can have colors mixed for you right in the store. Also, it is easier to work with than acrylic paint, going on smoother and more evenly and requiring less maintenance.

Acrylic paint should be reserved for small applications, such as the decorative elements of a design, as opposed to the basecoat, which should be applied using latex paint. Please note that when using acrylics, you will probably have to mix it with a little water, due to the thickness of the paint. You'll want your basecoat to be thinner (with the consistency of ordinary latex interior paint), while paint for smaller patterns—like the polka dots in the Polka-Dot Whimsy project on page 144 and the stars in its variation—can be worked without watering down the paint at all.

When the piece is ready, place it on a drop cloth. You can use the plastic type available in any hardware store, or try an old sheet—at least for the sanding phase. When you're done with sanding, you'll be grateful to wrap the residue up and throw it away—and not break out the vacuum. Whatever material you are working with, the sanding phase is an integral part of the process. For all types of wood, you'll want to use a medium to fine-grit sandpaper—150 grit is best—to get the piece smooth and ready for painting. Too coarse a grit will score the surface, while too fine a grit will not achieve the required smoothness. You can sand the piece by hand, or use an electric sander, which will save a lot of time.

After you've completely sanded the piece, run your hand along it, looking for bumps and splinters. When you're satisfied with the smoothness of the surface, wipe away residue with a damp cloth or a tack cloth. Once this phase is completed, remove the drop cloth you used for sanding and replace it with a clean one for painting. While some projects don't require a piece to be primed before you begin painting, most will benefit from at least one coat of primer. For the projects in this book, we used a water-based primer. A water-based primer is not only easier to clean from brushes, it also dries faster. Paint the entire piece of furniture with primer and allow each coat of primer to dry for at least two hours. Once the primer is dry, proceed with the base coat. Then follow the directions for the project you have chosen.

Brushes

You should have a variety of brushes of different sizes, thicknesses, shapes, and materials on hand before beginning a painted furniture project.

Sponge brushes are great for high-coverage projects—for painting primer and base coats. Depending on what you are painting, a 2- to 3-inch (5 to 8 cm) sponge brush will probably do the trick. The best part about sponge brushes is that they are inexpensive and disposable—no clean-up needed. Also, for projects that require a very smooth surface, such as the Mediterranean Lacquer piece on page 97, you don't have to worry about bristle marks—or stray bristles. They create smooth, even strokes.

BASIC MATERIALS

These are some of the basic tools you will need to create the projects and patterns in this book. Most of the materials are available through art-supply stores and craft shops, and some also can be found in paint and hardware stores.

Fluid acrylic paint Water-based paint that is ideal for decorative painting techniques. Due to its fluidity, it creates a marvelous glaze when mixed with glazing liquid. Mix glaze colors for custom effects, using primary colors plus white, black, and burnt umber.

Glazing liquid Water-based medium that can be mixed with fluid acrylic paint to increase the drying time. Fluid Acrylics work well for glaze colors because they have a very thin consistency and strong pigment characteristics. They are designed to mix well with Acrylic Glazing Liquid, producing outstanding transparent effects.

Glaze formula Mix three parts glazing liquid with one part fluid acrylic paint. This formula works well for the projects featured, but you may need to make adjustments based on the climate. For example, the paint might dry faster in warm temperatures, so you may need to add more glazing liquid.

Color Shapers, Wide Collection

Brushes Use a soft-bristle wash brush, 1" or 2" (25 mm or 50 mm), to apply the glaze. A stiff brush is not recommended because the rough bristles will not produce a smooth, even glaze. Foam brushes work well for priming and base-coating.

Sandpaper An assortment of grades are used in this book, including #400 wet or dry sandpaper (for sanding between coats of primer and base coat in the preparation process) and #600 wet or dry sandpaper (used in the finishing/wet-sanding process).

Palette paper Poly-coated paper for acrylics, with a slippery, waxy surface that is ideal for practicing color-shaping techniques, experimenting with strokes, and serving as a background on which to apply wet glaze.

Base-coat paint Interior latex semigloss paints or fluid acrylic paints work well for base-coating wood, wallpaper, vinyl, etc. Use interior latex semigloss for wall surfaces.

Water-based varnish, satin or semigloss This is used in all the projects—as a sealer between layers of paint; to prepare the surface before color shaping (a minimum of two coats are needed to produce an appropriately slick surface); and as a finish over the completed project (several coats are needed, and each coat should be allowed to dry thoroughly).

Primer Used to prepare the surface of unfinished wood before base-coat color is applied.

Quilter's pencil Ideal for marking patterns on the work surface. The pencil's markings are water-soluble, so the lines can be removed with a dampened paper towel.

SURFACE PREPARATION

Wood Surfaces

Surface preparation is the first step in the decorative painting process. Depending on the type of surface, different steps will apply. For example, unfinished wood needs to be sanded, sealed, and primed before base-coating. If your surface is already painted and in good condition, you may only need to sand the painted surface for good paint adhesion. If old paint or varnish is blistered, try a stripping product.

Prepare unfinished wood by first sanding it to a smooth finish, beginning with a medium-grade sandpaper (#150) and progressing to fine (#400).

Unfinished wood is porous and must be sealed or primed. Most paint-supply stores carry a number of very good sealer/primer products. Sometimes priming will raise the grain of the wood slightly. Sand between coats of sealer/primer with #400 sandpaper to smooth the grain of the wood.

Next, apply the base coat. Several coats are recommended. Sand between base coats to produce a quality finish. If you are working on large home-interior projects, use a good-quality semigloss latex paint. Use fluid acrylics, which are available in smaller quantities, for smaller projects. Unless directed otherwise, seal the base coat with water-based varnish to produce a slippery, protective layer. Now the surface is ready to color shape.

Wall Preparation

Walls also require preparation. The wall surface should be dust-free, primed, and painted with a interior latex semigloss paint. Finally, apply a coat of semigloss water-based varnish to protect the surface.

FINISHING

Varnishing completed projects enhances the finished work; the clear finish brings the colors in the patterns to life. Depending on the project, try increasing the number of varnish and wet-sand coats for a highly polished surface. Varnishing also protects the surface, making it functional.

Finishing Painted Wood Surfaces

Follow these steps to finish furniture and wooden objects.

1. When the finished painted design is completely dry, apply three coats of water-based varnish with a soft-bristle wash brush, using a gentle touch. Dry thoroughly between coats. Note: Placing too much pressure on the brush when varnishing could cause bubbles to form.

2. Wet-sanding with #600 wet or dry sandpaper smoothes any imperfections in the finished surface and prepares it for subsequent layers of varnish. Cut a piece of #600 wet or dry sandpaper, dip it into water, coat it with a little soap (the soap prevents scratching), and gently rub it over the decorated surface. It is important to use a light touch; don't rub aggressively. Remove the soapy film with a damp paper towel, and allow to air-dry. Varnish and wet-sand again. Repeat this process until the surface is perfectly smooth (on average, four or five times, but more if the desired effect calls for it).

3. Apply the final coat of varnish. Do not wet-sand after the final coat. You may leave the sheen from the final coat of gloss or satin varnish, or you may choose to rub the surface very gently in a circular motion with #0000 steel wool for an eggshell finish (but let the final coat of varnish dry overnight before beginning the rubbing process).

Finishing Walls and Wallpaper Borders

To produce a functional surface, finish walls and wallpaper borders with one or two coats of water-based varnish.

This Beach Cabana Bureau is perfect for a seaside cottage—or even for an urban space decorated to suggest a home by the sea. In this relatively easy project, only the drawer fronts are painted. The natural exposed pine calls to mind the boardwalk at the beach, while the playful colorful stripes echo umbrellas, beach balls, and care-free summer days.

beach cabana *bureau*

Materials

- Screwdriver to match screws holding drawer pulls.
- Extra-fine sandpaper
- Tack cloth
- Three paint brushes: one 3-inch (7.5 cm) wide for primer and base coat; one 5/8-inch (1.5 cm) flat art brush for painting stripes; one 5/16-inch (8 mm) flat art brush for touch-ups
- One small can of water-based primer
- One small can of water-based, flat-finish, bright white paint
- Ruler
- T-square
- Roll of 7/8-inch (2 cm) painter's masking tape
- Three small cans of water-based, flat-finish paint: one country blue; one apple red; one navy blue
- One spray can of polyurethane satin finish

TIP

When working with pine, you may have to contend with knots. Generally, the primer will cover these. For really stubborn knots, apply wood filler to the knot and sand carefully before applying the primer.

Method

- Study the photo on the facing page. Simply by careful measuring, masking, and painting you can transform a plain pine dresser into this perky cabana-style piece. Before you start, practice on scrap pieces of plywood or like surface.

- Be sure to cut each piece of masking tape long enough so that it overhangs each side. This will make it easier to pull off.

- Take care that the masking tape is straight and free of air bubbles on the drawer fronts. While a slightly imperfect line will give the piece charm, rough, jagged or blurred lines just look messy.

- Do not paint completely over the tape, as this will make the tape more difficult to remove.

- Also note that you will need ten to twelve hours to complete the project. Perform steps 1 through 3 on all drawer fronts before proceeding. Steps 4 through 6 should be completed within four hours to avoid problems removing the masking tape.

PAINTING SURFACE
A three-drawer dresser in unfinished pine (other light woods will work just as well)

PATTERN
None required

COMPLETION TIME
Twelve hours (including drying time)

RATING

starting *out*

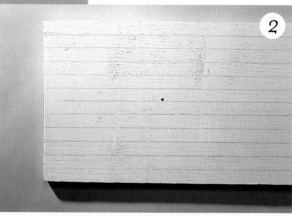

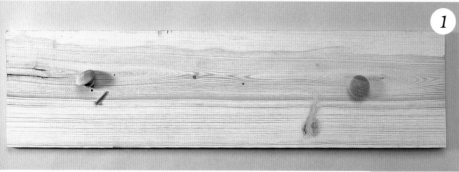

Step 1 Remove drawers from dresser. Unscrew knobs from drawers and put aside. Sand down the drawer fronts one at a time. Wipe with tack cloth to remove residue. Apply primer to each drawer front. Using the widest brush, paint with the grain of the wood. Allow first coat to dry for at least two hours. Paint over the primer coat with the bright white base coat, painting with the grain.

Step 2 Line up the ruler on the left side of the drawer front, working with one drawer at a time. With pencil, mark 7/8-inch (2 cm) increments. Using the T-square, draw light pencil lines across the drawer fronts at these increments.

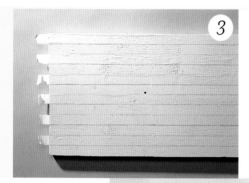

Step 3 Line up strips of masking tape just above the bottom of every other line. Make sure the masking tape strips extend about an inch beyond each side of the drawer. This will make it easier to pull them off. Important: manufacturers recommend removing the tape within four hours, so apply only to drawers you will be painting right away. Do not place masking tape until basecoat is completely dry.

Step 4 Select a paint color for the first drawer. With a 5/8-inch (1.5 cm) flat art brush, paint lightly and evenly over the exposed sections of the drawer front. Do not paint completely over the tape or it will be sealed to the drawer. A heavy coat of paint will make the tape brittle and difficult to peel and might cause the color to bleed under the tape, ruining the striped effect. Apply two coats of paint, allowing each to dry for at least forty-five minutes.

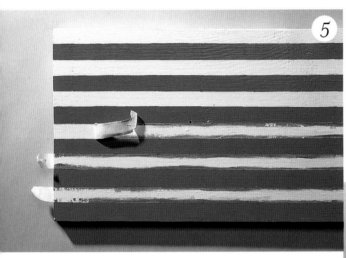

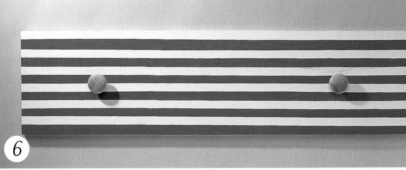

Step 5 Gently peel off the masking tape, row by row. Important: manufacturers recommend removing the tape within four hours, so for best results, remove masking tape as soon as the second color coat dries. Touch up uneven areas with a 5/16-inch (8 mm) flat art brush. Repeat steps 4 through 6 with remaining drawer fronts.

Step 6 Apply polyurethane finish. Two coats are recommended. When drawer front is completely dry, reattach drawer pulls.

variation

For a more complicated variation, try wider or even vertical stripes. Or, paint waves on the drawers instead of straightforward stripes. Check craft and notions stores for beach-themed stencils or decals, and instead of taking the stripes the whole way across on one drawer, paint a seashell on that end.

Method

Create irregular stripes in soft colors with a subtractive method of decorative painting. Prepare drawer fronts as in steps 1 and 2 using icy blue instead of bright white for the basecoat. Apply a thin coat of accent color and remove by wiping the wet paint with the cardboard strips to create a striped pattern revealing the base coat below.

TIP

Make sure your accent color is not thinned so much that it runs, and work quickly so that it does not set before you use the cardboard strips. If you make a mistake, you can wipe it off with a clean rag and start again.

Materials

- Two cardboard strips, 1 3/4 inches (4 cm) wide and 5/8 inch (1.5 cm) wide.
- Base coat color, icy blue latex semigloss
- Accent color, citrus yellow latex semigloss

- Fine sandpaper
- Tack cloth to remove dust
- Three paintbrushes: one 2-inch (5 cm) wide for primer and base coat; one ¼" (6 mm) round artist's brush for painting polka dots; and one ¹⁄₁₆" (1.5 mm) round artist's brush for touch-ups
- One small can of latex-based primer
- A number-two pencil
- One small container of acrylic paint, in olive green*
- One small can container of acrylic paint, in peach*
- One small can container of acrylic paint, in periwinkle*
- One spray can satin-finish polyurethane

*Note: You will need a larger container of paint in the color you choose to paint the rest of the piece.

PAINTING SURFACE
An unfinished pine bureau

PATTERN
A quarter or other coin in the size of your choice

COMPLETION TIME
Ten hours
(including drying time)

RATING

Make an ordinary dresser the focal piece of a room—it just takes a bit of color and a simple pattern. This dresser, with its brightly colored drawer fronts and playful polka dots, could easily be at home in a kid's room or in the master bedroom.

polka-dot *whimsy*

TIP

Instead of tracing the coin over and over on the drawer front, trace it many times on a piece of cardboard. Cut out the coin shapes, and lay them over the drawer front in the pattern shown on page 147, or in one of your choosing. This will provide a complete visual before the dresser gets marked up. Trace the dots onto the drawer front and proceed with the project as follows.

Method

- Before you begin, study the photo on the opposite page. This project requires sanding, priming, and painting with a pattern you can easily master. Experiment with your technique on a piece of scrap wood before you get to the actual piece.

- You don't have to use a quarter. For bigger polka dots, you can try a silver dollar; for smaller ones, a nickel or a penny might make your best choice.

- Take your time and paint in the polka dots with care. While you can touch-up either color once you've finished, it's better—and easier—to get it right the first time.

starting *out*

Remove drawers from dresser. Unscrew knobs from drawers and put aside. Sand down the drawer fronts one at a time and then sand down dresser. Wipe with a tack cloth to remove residue. Apply primer to each drawer front with the 2 inch (5 cm) brush. Paint with the grain of the wood. Allow first coat to dry, and, if needed, apply a second coat and allow to dry for an additional two hours.

1

Step 1 Following the grain of the wood, paint over the primer coat on one of the drawer fronts with the olive green base coat, using the 2-inch (5 cm) brush. Let dry. Apply a second coat and let dry.

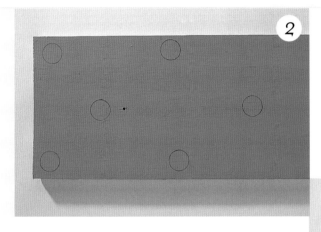

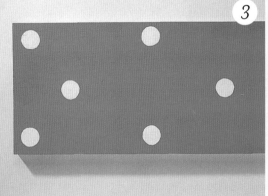

Step 2 Arrange coins or cardboard cutouts on drawer front, playing around with position until you find the most appealing arrangement, or follow the arrangement provided in the photo on page 145. With pencil, trace the polka-dot templates, pressing firmly so you can clearly see the outlines.

Step 3 Taking the ¹⁄₄" (6 mm) round paintbrush, fill in the polka dots with the peach paint. Touch-up uneven areas with a ¹⁄₁₆ " (1.5 mm) round artist's brush. Repeat steps 1 through 3 with remaining drawer fronts, using the periwinkle as a base coat for one and the peach as a base coat for the other. Here, the olive green-colored drawer has peach polka dots, but you can use the blue if you choose. Just limit your color choices to a total of three to give the piece a sense of unity.

TIP

Experiment with different ways to apply paint. Instead of using the traditional bristle or sponge brush, try ragging on paint or applying with a sea sponge for a completely different effect.

Step 4 Apply polyurethane finish to drawer fronts. Two coats are recommended. When drawer fronts are completely dry, reattach knobs. Apply a coat of primer to the dresser frame. Allow to dry for two hours, and apply a second coat, which should dry for an additional two hours. Paint the remainder of the dresser in olive, peach, or periwinkle, and be sure to paint two coats all around. We chose olive, but your décor may call for one of the other colors to be emphasized. Apply two coats of polyurethane finish, and allow the piece to dry overnight.

variation

whimsy

Not a fan of polka dots? Create star, moon, heart, shell, or whatever-shape-you-like templates. Check craft and notions stores for stencils or decals. For larger shapes, try cookie cutters. Find whimsical knobs and drawer pulls in housewares stores to complete your theme. This is a simple variation that sets the theme of bright stars on a night sky.

Method

Follow the directions for Polka-Dot Whimsy on pages 146–148, this time substituting new colors and the star templates for the polka dots. Trace star template on page 257 onto tracing paper. Carefully cut out template drawn on tracing paper and trace onto oak tag. Create several templates—so you can lay them out across your drawer—and carefully cut out. Proceed as directed.

TIP

Get inspiration from the other design elements in the room where you plan to put the dresser. Is there any one element that could be tied into the dresser? How about the finials on the curtain rods or an interesting shade pull? Is there a wallpaper border with a simple shape you could pick up and echo on the dresser?

Materials

Have the same materials on hand for the variation, but include the following:

- A sheet of tracing paper to trace star template
- A number-two pencil
- One sheet of oak tag or thin, clean cardboard
- One small container of acrylic paint, in aquamarine
- One small container of acrylic paint, in bright yellow
- Small containers of acrylic paint for the other colors you'll introduce for the other drawers and the dresser itself

Life's a party, so add a little fiesta to your kitchen, living room, even bedroom. This vibrantly patterned project is a perfect complement to an already colorful room (as shown) but can also be a welcome splash of color in an otherwise plain décor. The bright colors aren't typical of southwestern style, but the patterns make an undeni-able southwestern statement.

Materials

- Screwdriver to match cabinet-hardware screws
- Fine sandpaper
- Tack cloth to remove dust
- One small can of latex-based primer
- One 2-inch (5 cm) brush; one 1/2-inch (1 cm) flat art brush; one 1/4-inch (6 mm) flat art brush
- One small can of water-based primer
- T-square (optional)
- 12- or 18-inch (30 cm or 46 cm) ruler
- One roll of 1-inch-wide (3 cm) painter's masking tape
- One small container of acrylic paint, in cadmium red (ready-made)
- One small container of acrylic paint, in cobalt blue (ready-made)
- One small container of acrylic paint, in sky blue
- One small container of acrylic paint, in bright green
- One small container of acrylic paint, in bright orange
- One small container of acrylic paint, in cadmium yellow, medium (ready-made)
- One spray can satin-finish polyurethane

southwestern *fiesta*

PAINTING SURFACE
An unfinished pine cabinet

PATTERN
A series of templates (found on pages 258–260)

COMPLETION TIME
Twenty-four hours (including drying time)

RATING /////

TIP

You can use a T-square to line up the placement of your stripes, but you may find that a 12-inch or 18-inch (30 cm or 46 cm) ruler is more manageable.

Method

- This piece is all about pattern and color. With its carefully drawn templates, a little masking tape, and a rainbow of colors, it's challenging and time consuming—but well worth the effort. This project demonstrates the pattern on the lower section of the cabinet doors. Pattern templates for this section, as well as the top sections, are available on pages 258–260.

- Practice drawing and coloring in these templates on oak tag or ideally, on scrap pieces of wood before you work on the cabinet. The colors in this cabinet are very rich and vibrant, and the fewer mistakes you make, the less tedious the touch-up work.

- If you are working on a cabinet, remove the doors. The pattern will be much easier to execute flat.

- Always work on the patterned sections before painting the unpatterned sections of your piece. You can always work on these sections while your patterned pieces are drying between steps.

starting *out*

Trace and cut out templates on pages 258–260 and set aside. Remove doors from cabinet. Unscrew any knobs or hardware and put them aside. Sand down the cabinet doors one at a time. Sand the remainder of the cabinet. Wipe with a tack cloth to remove residue. With the 2-inch (5 cm) brush, apply primer to each cabinet door, back side first, and allow to dry. Paint with the grain of the wood. Allow first coat to dry for at least two hours. If needed, apply a second coat and allow to dry for an additional two hours.

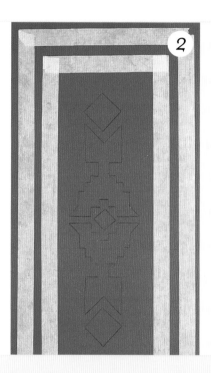

Step 1 With 2-inch (5 cm) brush, paint the back side of the cabinet door in the bright red paint, and allow to dry for at least an hour. Once dry, lay the backside down on a clean old sheet and proceed to paint the front sides in bright red, with the grain. Allow first coat to dry for at least two hours, and paint a second coat of bright red. Allow base coat to dry overnight.

Step 2 With a ruler or T-square, measure the width of the cabinet doors, measuring in from the outside edges of the cabinet doors. Precisely where you decide to put your stripes will depend on the width of your doors. (We measured in 4 inches [10 cm].) Mark these points with a number-two pencil. Take your T-square or ruler and lightly draw in lines to mark the position of your masking tape. Line the masking tape up along the inner perimeter of your pencil lines, making a rectangle. With your ruler, measure out from this inside rectangle about 1 inch (3 cm). Mark these points with the number-two pencil, then with your ruler or T-square, draw lines to mark the position of your outer masking tape rectangle.

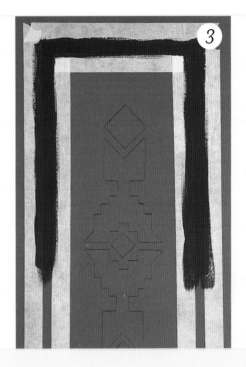

Step 3 Once you've established the position of your border, experiment with the placement of your templates. You can use a ruler to designate equal distances for top and bottom and right and left placement. Once you have your templates in place, trace them onto the board with the number-two pencil. With the 1/2-inch (1 cm) flat art brush, paint the border in cobalt blue, trying not to paint too much over the masking tape itself, as this will make the tape difficult to remove. Allow to dry for about twenty minutes then, paint a second coat.

(Note: If you are using acrylic paint, do not thin the blue paint.)

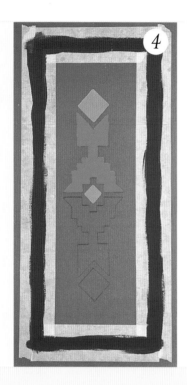

Step 4 With the ¼-inch (6 mm) flat art brush, paint in the template, using sky blue for the diamonds and bright green for the other shapes. (Note: If you are using acrylic paint, you should thin the bright green and sky blue paint to a fluid consistency.) Allow to dry for about one hour.

Step 5 Carefully remove the masking tape. Touch-up the door as necessary. Apply polyurethane finish to front and back of cabinet doors. Two coats are recommended. Using the picture on page 150 as your guide, repeat these steps for the remaining cabinet doors. See pages 258–260 for remaining templates.

variation

fiesta

For a more traditional southwestern feel, use the same patterns, but substitute pastel colors for the bold red and blue used in the original piece. Depending on the shape of your cabinet, you can use this pattern layout on the horizontal, or get really creative and vary the order and direction of the patterns.

Method

This variation is performed in the same way as the original project, using different colors. Because it may be difficult to see pencil over the dark purple basecoat, try tracing the template with white chalk. You can easily see it and whatever you don't paint over will simply wipe away once the piece is dry.

TIP

Keep in mind, you don't have to use these colors if others are more appealing to you. If you do choose other colors, please be sure to consult color directories, however, to make sure the ones you have selected will work well together. As an added precaution, you can actually paint the color scheme together on a piece of scrap wood before you begin.

Materials

Have the same materials on hand for the variation, but include the following:
- One small container of acrylic paint, in lavender
- One small container of acrylic paint, in coral pink

- Fine sandpaper
- Tack cloth
- Ruler
- Number-two pencil
- Chalk (optional)
- Masking tape
- Three paintbrushes: one 2-inch (5 cm) sponge brush for applying primer and base coat; one 1/4-inch (6 mm) round art brush for leaves; one 1/8-inch (3 mm) round liner brush for painting in vine and touch-ups
- One small can of water-based primer
- One small can of water-based, flat paint in pale sage green for basecoat
- One small can of water-based, flat paint in jasper green for vine
- One spray can satin-finish polyurethane

PAINTING SURFACE
An unfinished pine dresser

PATTERN
None required

COMPLETION TIME
Four hours
(including drying time)

RATING //

Swedish colors are light and pastel, and that's the secret to creating the ultimate Swedish piece. In this project, we transformed a plain wooden table into a vanity by adding a simple apron to three sides. The piece is then finished with a pale mint–green color creates a delightful backdrop for a simple vine pattern.

swedish *lights*

Method

- This simple vine pattern requires only a few careful brush-strokes, but it's a good idea to practice your technique a few times before painting the finished piece.

- Try to paint the vine freehand, or mark a pattern lightly in pencil or chalk to follow.

- For a more elaborate effect, paint the vine motif on, or around, the table's legs.

starting *out*

Sand the table and remove any residue with tack cloth or slightly damp cloth. With the 2-inch (5 cm) brush, apply the first coat of primer. Allow top to dry thoroughly and apply the second coat.

Step 1 Use a jigsaw to cut a wooden apron to fit around the back outside edge of the table. If you don't want to do this yourself, you may be able to have the wood cut for you at a home improvement store. Just bring a template.

Step 2 Secure the apron in place with strong wood glue. Drill through both layers to create a starter hole, then attach the apron firmly with wood screws.

With the 2-inch (5 cm) brush, apply two coats of primer to the table, allowing coats to dry thoroughly in between. With the 2-inch (5 cm) brush, paint the table completely in the light sage green base coat. Let dry thoroughly and apply a second coat.

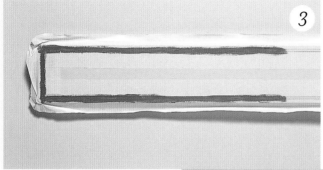

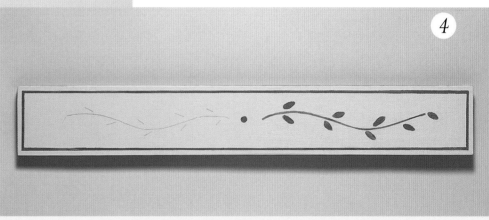

Step 3 With a ruler, measure in 1/2 inch (1 cm) from the edges of the front of table and mark with pencil or chalk. Mask off and paint border in jasper green with the 1/4 inch (1 cm) round artist's brush. Carefully remove masking tape upon completion. Allow paint to dry thoroughly before moving to the next step.

Step 4 If you are more comfortable doing so, draw in the vine pattern lightly in pencil or in chalk. With the 1/8-inch (6 mm) round liner brush, paint in vine pattern, following the photo on page 157.

5

TIP

Flat-finish paint gives a soft effect perfect for Swedish design as well as Colonial-style rooms and the like. The main problem with flat-finish paint, however, is that it is difficult to clean and should only be used on items that don't get a lot of wear and tear. An alternative for a piece in a high-volume area is eggshell finish. It is barely reflective, so you can keep a subdued appearance, but is much easier to clean.

Step 5 Create a central floral motif as a centerpiece to two vines by painting four leaf shapes around a center dot. When the table is completely dry, spray with polyurethane top coat and let dry thoroughly.

variation

This variation mimics the original pattern, except that the pattern is more detailed and controlled. The antique white backdrop sets a delicate feel, perfect for a woman's vanity or dressing table. For a country look, change the colors. Try painting a blue leaf pattern over a beige background.

Method

This variation is performed in much the same way as the preceding project, but in this case, a tiny leaf shape was created, cut out, and traced around the vine, making for a more precise effect. First prime the table. Then paint two coats of the antique white basecoat. Once the basecoat has dried, create the border. Next, lightly draw in the vine with pencil or white chalk. Next, trace leaf shapes around the vine, following photo. Paint in vine using liner brush and leaves with round art brush.

Materials

- Fine sandpaper
- Tack cloth
- Ruler
- Number-two pencil
- Chalk (optional)
- Masking tape
- Three paint brushes: one 2-inch (5 cm) sponge brush for applying primer and base coat; one 1/4-inch (6 mm) round art brush for leaves; one 1/8-inch (3 mm) round liner brush for painting in vine and touch-ups
- One small can of water-based primer
- One small can of water-based, flat paint in antique white for basecoat
- One small can of water-based, flat paint in jasper green for vine
- One spray can satin-finish polyurethane

Bring a mod, retro feel into a living space with this cabinet, which features bold, brash, and bright colors and cool circle shapes. This cabinet is different than other projects in this book as it is done with spray paint on metal. Using a high-gloss spray paint ensures a true-to-life metallic finish.

Materials

- Fine-grit sandpaper
- Several large sheets of oak tag or lightweight cardboard
- Compass (optional)
- One can of water-based spray primer
- One can of spray paint, in apple red gloss
- Low-tack double-sided tape
- A roll of painter's masking tape
- One can of spray paint, in orange gloss
- One can of spray paint, in orange-yellow gloss
- One can of spray paint, in magenta gloss
- One spray can gloss-finish polyurethane

seventies chic cabinet

TIP

When using spray paint, always work in a well-ventilated area. The best bet is to work outside, if possible. If working outside, make sure it's a still day. Any wind can cause particles to stick to wet paint. Keep in mind, however, that spray paint will crackle and peel in temperatures below 50°F.

Method

- For the best effect, create circles in different sizes. You can do this using the templates on page 262 or by using a compass to determine the sizes you want. Large circles are best for this project.

- Make sure the surface is completely smooth and free of any dust or dirt before painting.

- Allow coats of paint to dry thoroughly before moving on to the next step.

- Ensure that stencils are securely applied to the surface and that there are no gaps or tears in the stencil before painting so that paint will not get outside the circles. For best results, apply the low-tack double-sided tape to the inner edge of the circle to prevent paint from seeping under the stencil. Use masking tape as a secondary way to secure the stencil and to keep it from blowing around during spraying.

PAINTING SURFACE
A metal cabinet

PATTERN
A series of stencils (found on pages 262–263)

COMPLETION TIME
Thirty hours (including drying time)

RATING ////

starting *out*

Lightly sand the cabinet's surface to dull down the slick original finish. This allows the paint to adhere to the metal surface better, since paint easily peals from a slick surface. After sanding, clean with a slightly damp cloth. Spray with two light coats of primer. Trace stencils from page 262 onto oak tag or lightweight cardboard and cut out circle shapes. Set aside.

TIP

To bring out the inherent shininess of metal, it's a good idea to paint it with a high-gloss finish. The drawback of this type of finish, however, is that it will show every flaw, no matter how carefully you sand. Try painting in a semi-gloss finish and use a high-gloss topcoat.

1

Step 1 After letting the primer dry, spray on the red base coat. Let dry thoroughly and apply a second coat.

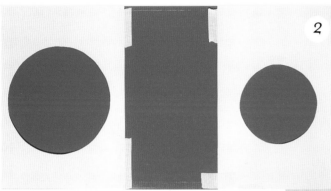

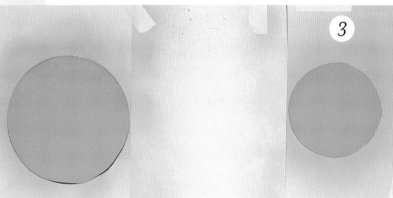

Step 2 Position stencils on the cabinet and secure the inner edges with low-tack double-sided tape and the outer edges with masking tape.

Step 3 Spray additional colors.

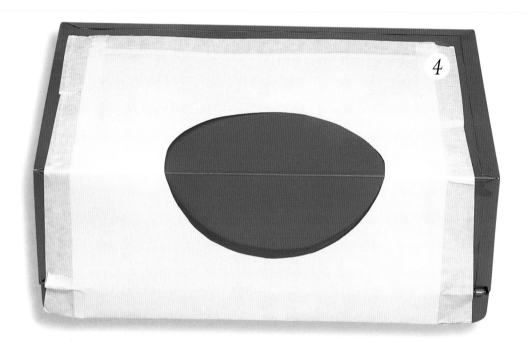

Step 4 To do corners or edges, bend stencils over side of cabinet and tape in place. Spray over the template. Spray the cabinet with gloss polyurethane top coat and let dry.

variation

cabinet

This variation features new shapes (templates on page 263) and bright colors: blue and yellow.

Method

Follow the directions on pages 164 to 166 to create this variation. Be sure to create stencils of all different sizes for a funky effect. These shapes will be trickier to work with than the standard circle stencil, so be sure to give yourself ample practice time—especially for shapes that drape over the top and sides of your cabinet.

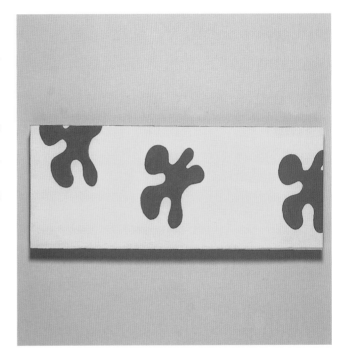

Materials

- Fine sandpaper
- Several large sheets of oak tag or lightweight cardboard
- One can of water-based spray primer
- One can of spray paint, in bright yellow gloss
- Low-tack, double-sided tape
- A roll of painter's masking tape
- One can of spray paint, in bright blue gloss
- One can clear satin spray varnish

Blue and white are right at home in a country décor and potted–plant motifs evoke garden images that work just as well in a weekend cottage as they do in an urban space. Distressing the dining set gives it a timeworn casual effect. This project focuses on completing the chair. However, the table legs use the same template as the chair backs.

Materials

- Fine and medium grit sandpaper
- Tack cloth
- Three paintbrushes: one 2-inch (5 cm) sponge brush for base coat, one $^1/_{16}$-inch (1.5 mm) round liner brush for border, and one $^1/_8$-inch (3 mm) round artist's brush for potted-plant shapes
- One small can of flat-finish latex paint, in blossom white
- One small can of flat-finish latex paint, in deep blue
- Number-two pencil
- Roll of 1-inch (2.5 cm) painter's masking tape
- One spray can satin-finish polyurethane

country *heritage*

TIP

If you are working with a light-toned wood, stain the pieces first in walnut or similarly dark-toned wood stain to make the distressing effect more prominent.

Method

- The potted-plant shapes of this project are large enough that you should be able to paint them in without a problem. However, it never hurts to practice.

- Depending on your skill and confidence level, you may be more comfortable using a stencil. This means that instead of cutting the shapes out and tracing them, you will be using the piece of oak tag you cut the shape out of.

- Paint border in completely freehand, or use masking tape or the edge of the template to paint straight lines for the inside straight border.

PAINTING SURFACE
An unfinished walnut dining set

PATTERN
A potted-plant template and border template (found on pages 264–265)

COMPLETION TIME
Eight hours (including drying time)

RATING //

starting *out*

Sand down the dining set with fine-grit sandpaper and remove residue with tack cloth. Trace and cut out templates on pages 264-266 and set aside. Do not use primer for this project.

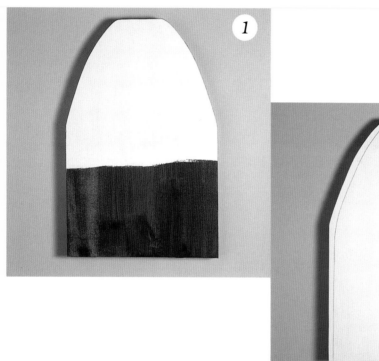

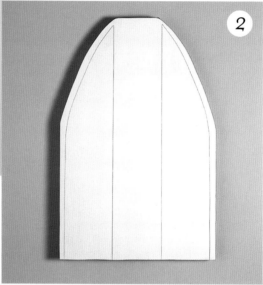

Step 1 With the 2-inch (5 cm) sponge brush, paint the dining set in two coats of the white base coat, allowing the first coat to dry thoroughly before painting the second.

Step 2 Line up border templates on chair back. With number-two pencil, trace templates onto chair.

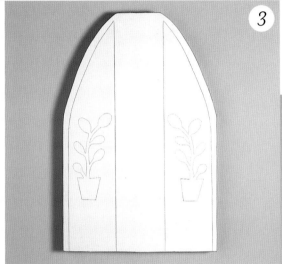

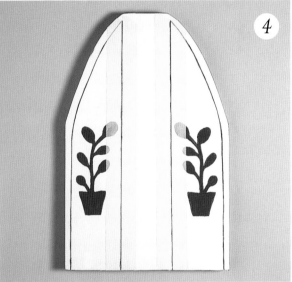

Step 3 Center potted-plant templates within borders, following the photo above. Keeping these in place, trace onto chairback with number-two pencil.

Step 4 With the 1/8-inch (3 mm) round artist's brush and the deep blue paint, carefully paint in the potted-plant templates. Allow to dry thoroughly. With the 1/16-inch (1.5 mm) round liner brush, carefully paint in the borders. If desired, line up masking tape on either side of inner borders and paint within masking tape lines to ensure straight line. Remove the tape immediately after painting. Allow piece to dry overnight.

Step 5 With the sandpaper, gently distress the chair—focusing on the white portions and not the blue. Brush away any residue, spray with polyurethane and let dry.

variation

Select other typical country shapes to lend a rural elegance to furniture. In this case, red hearts set a distinctly country-casual mood. Other simple typically country shapes you may choose to try out instead are butterflies, daisies and other uncomplicated floral shapes, garden tools, trees, and barns. Find a picture of one of these shapes and trace over it with tracing paper to create your own stencil—or try sketching freehand if you are feeling adventurous.

Materials and Method

Use the same materials for this variation, substituting the heart templates on page 266 for the potted plants and the colonial red paint for the deep blue. You can choose to distress the piece or not, depending on your personal preference. The country feel will come through on its own, with the colors and shapes chosen. Proceed with project following directions on pages 170–171.

- Medium and fine grit sandpaper
- Tack cloth
- One 2-inch (5 cm) sponge brush for all applications
- One can of water-based primer
- One small can of satin-finish latex paint, in wildflower blue
- One small can of satin-finish latex paint, in colonial red
- Number-two pencil
- Ruler
- A piece of white chalk
- Roll of 2-inch (5 cm) painter's masking tape
- One spray can satin-finish polyurethane

A harlequin pattern is a classic motif that adds style to any décor. The colors chosen for this project lend the piece a decided country flair, but you don't have to be locked into that. Change the feel by using pinks and greens for a traditional harlequin pattern, black and silver for a high-tech mood—whatever colors you choose, the pattern should translate.

PAINTING SURFACE
A well-weathered pine table

PATTERN
No templates required

COMPLETION TIME
Twelve to fifteen hours (including drying time)

RATING //

classic motif

Method

- This easy project doesn't require any templates. To complete it, you simply measure lines and paint within the borders.

- Use chalk to draw in lines. It's easy to rub away once the piece is completed and you won't have to worry about covering up pencil lines.

- Start with the blue as your base coat, and paint red over the blue. Typically, it's easier to paint a dark color over a light color rather than the other way around. While in this case, both colors are equally dark, blue is an easier color to paint over than red.

- Try lining up masking tape on the lines before you paint to ensure clean, straight edges.

starting *out*

With fine grit sandpaper sand down the table and remove residue with tack cloth.

Paint the table with two coats of primer.

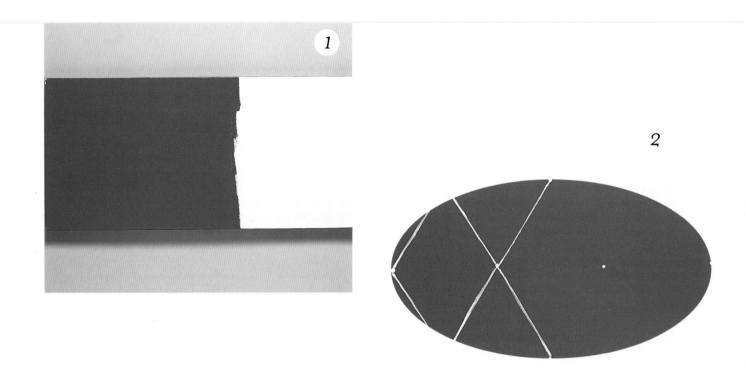

Step 1   With the 2-inch (5 cm) brush, paint the table in two coats of the wildflower blue base coat, allowing the first coat to dry thoroughly before applying the second.

Step 2   With the ruler and chalk, measure and mark placement of diamond shapes on tabletop or other surface. Draw in the lines with white chalk.

3

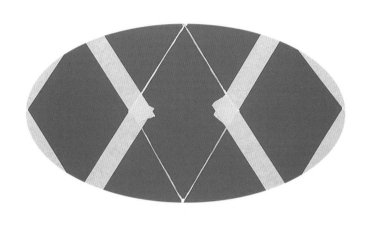

4

Step 3 Line up masking tape on the outside edges of the diamonds that are being painted red. You will only be able to paint the outer two diamonds first. Once they are dry, you can mask off and paint the center diamond.

Step 4 Paint the designated diamonds in colonial red with the 2-inch (5 cm) sponge brush. Carefully peel the tape off before the paint dries to avoid having it dry to the surface. Once the paint has completely dried, repeat the process with the center diamond.

5

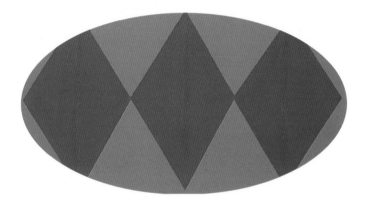

Step 5 Allow the piece to dry overnight. The next morning, distress the table with medium grit sandpaper. For best results, distress only the diamonds, allowing the wildflower blue base coat to shine through.

Step 6 When piece is thoroughly dry, spray with satin-finish polyurethane top coat and let dry.

variation

A checkerboard pattern, with its clean lines and symmetry, is another classic motif. You can do a tight pattern, such as the one we did, or use a larger grid for a cleaner, more open look. Also, we used three different shades of blue, but the effect will be just as strong with just two colors.

Method

Measure the piece to determine how many squares you'll need to allot, and how large they should be. Mark the lines and draw in with a ruler and chalk or pencil. Proceed with project following directions on pages 176–178.

Materials

- Medium and fine sandpaper
- Tack cloth
- One 2-inch (5 cm) sponge brush for all applications
- One can of water-based primer
- One small can of water-based, satin-finish paint in wildflower blue
- One small can of water-based, satin-finish paint in medium blue
- One small can of water-based, satin-finish paint in pale blue
- Number-two pencil
- Ruler
- A piece of white chalk
- Roll of 2-inch (5 cm) painter's masking tape
- One spray can satin-finish polyurethane

painting
surfaces and walls

AGATE SHELF

Faux agate, shown here in a limited palette of three colors, works well on surfaces such as a wooden shelf. Mark off sections of the shelf to suggest pieces of stone (this will also make it easier to control the glaze). Consider broadening your range of colors to include hues such as yellow ochre and deep violet-black.

MATERIALS

- unfinished wooden shelf
- sandpaper, assorted grades
- primer
- 2" (50mm) Flat Wide Color Shaper, cut, notched, and slit
- 1" (25mm) Flat Wide Color Shaper, cut, notched, and slit (optional)
- soft-bristle wash brush, 1" or 2"
- base-coat color, pink-beige (fluid acrylic paint) interior latex semigloss paint or
- glaze colors, light rust and deep rust fluid acrylic paint
- glazing liquid
- water-based varnish, satin or semigloss
- painter's tape
- plastic wrap

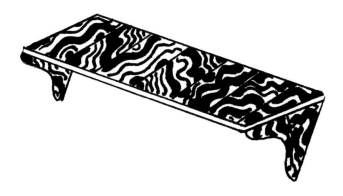

Starting Out *Sketch your project to develop the linear patterns. Cut, notch, and slit the Flat Wide Color Shaper.*

3" (77mm) Curve Color Shaper, cut, notched, and slit

1" (25mm) Curve Color Shaper, cut, notched, and slit

1

2

STEP 1 Follow instructions for preparing wood as directed in the Basic Materials section. Apply a base coat of pink-beige to the shelf (if you use acrylic paint for a base coat, seal the paint with one or two coats of semigloss varnish). Dry thoroughly.

STEP 2 Prepare glazes of light rust and deep rust by mixing three parts glazing liquid with one part fluid acrylic paint. For a clean-edged effect, section off and mask one area at a time with painter's tape. Apply light rust glaze diagonally in one direction. Immediately and gently apply the deep rust glaze diagonally in the opposite direction, softening the two colors by blending them.

STEP 3 Gently move your hand to form wavy, ribbon-like lines in the wet glaze with the 2" Flat Color Shaper, cut, notched, and slit. Linear patterns emerge from a single stroke. Dry thoroughly, and remove tape. Treat the entire surface, varying the linear pattern. Change the width of lines by using the 1" Flat Color Shaper, cut, notched, and slit. Wipe excess glaze from the Color Shaper as you proceed. Dry thoroughly, and seal with a coat of varnish.

3

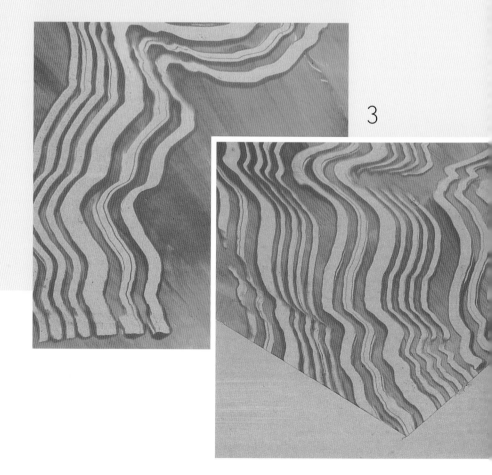

*Let each section dry thoroughly before tap-
ing off an adjacent area. Protect wet areas
by first treating sections that do not touch.*

4

STEP 4 Add texture by applying the same deep-rust glaze over
the entire patterned surface, placing plastic wrap over the wet glaze,
pressing it gently, and immediately peeling it off. Dry thoroughly, and
follow the finishing instructions in the Basic Materials section.

1

2

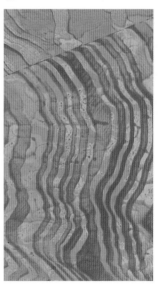

VARIATION *Add colors by over-glazing the completed pattern. This
pattern, for example, shows a yellow-ochre glaze applied
over the completed agate.*

STEP 1 Complete the agate pattern, and seal the completed pattern with
a coat of varnish. Dry thoroughly.

STEP 2 Prepare a glaze by mixing three parts glazing liquid with one part
yellow ochre. Create a multicolored effect by applying the glaze over random areas with a soft-bristle wash brush. Dry thoroughly, and follow the
finishing instructions in the Basic Materials section.

MALACHITE CHEST

Faux malachite lends itself to many surfaces, such as wood moldings, fireplaces, and accent pieces of furniture. Typically, faux stone patterns on such surfaces are large. The small wooden chest featured here shows malachite's intricate pattern covering the sides and top. Subdued tones of teal green replace the natural stone's deeper, brighter tones.

MATERIALS

- unfinished wooden chest
- sandpaper, assorted grades
- primer
- 2" (50mm) Flat Wide Color Shaper, cut, notched, and slit
- 1" (25mm) Flat Wide Color Shaper, cut, notched, and slit (optional)
- soft-bristle wash brush, 1" or 2"
- basecoat color, light mint-green (interior latex semigloss paint or) fluid acrylic paint
- glaze colors, sea-foam green and dark teal fluid acrylic paint
- glazing liquid
- water-based varnish, satin or semigloss
- painter's tape
- plastic wrap

3" (77mm) Curve Color Shaper, cut, notched, and slit

1" (25mm) Curve Color Shaper, cut, notched, and slit

Starting Out *Sketch your project to develop a pattern of lines and concentric rings. Mark the surface into sections to get a rough idea of how to lay out each section as a piece of stone. Cut, notch, and slit the Flat Wide Color Shaper.*

EXAMPLE STROKE

1

2

STEP 1 Follow instructions for preparing wood as directed in the Basic Materials section. Apply a base coat of light mint-green paint to the chest (if you use fluid acrylics for a base coat, seal the background color with one or two coats of varnish). Dry thoroughly.

STEP 2 Prepare glazes of sea-foam green and dark teal by mixing three parts glazing liquid with one part fluid acrylic paint. For a clean-edged and realistic effect, section off and mask one area at a time with painter's tape. The approach is similar to the agate process. Use a soft-bristle wash brush to apply the sea-foam green glaze in one diagonal direction. Immediately and gently apply the dark teal in the opposite direction, softening the two colors by blending them.

STEP 3 Form malachite's wavy, ribbonlike lines of undulating curves and concentric circles by dragging the 2" Flat Wide Color Shaper, cut, notched, and slit, through the wet glaze. Wipe excess glaze from the Color Shaper as you proceed. Incorporate more varied linear effects with a 1" Flat-Shaper. Dry thoroughly, and remove tape. Treat the entire surface. Dry thoroughly, and seal with a coat of varnish.

3

TIP

Dry each section thoroughly before taping off adjacent areas. Protect wet areas by first treating sections that do not touch. After they dry completely, line up the tape to treat adjacent sections.

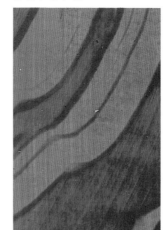 

VARIATION

Increase the intensity of the colors by adding a deeper, richer-colored glaze over the treated surface. The color changes without obscuring the patterns. The glazing liquid enhances transparency.

Seal the faux malachite surface with a coat of varnish. Prepare a deeper, more vibrant turquoise glaze by mixing three parts glazing liquid with one part teal. Use a soft-bristle wash brush to apply a layer of glaze over the entire surface. Dry thoroughly, and follow the finishing instructions in the Basic Materials section.

4

STEP 4 Add texture by applying a layer of dark-teal glaze over the entire patterned surface, placing plastic wrap over the wet glaze, pressing it gently, and immediately peeling it off. Dry thoroughly, and follow the finishing instructions in the Basic Materials section.

MARBLE TABLE

Many large objects offer good surfaces for faux marble—tabletops, accent areas on furniture, and interior woodwork such as door frames, window moldings, raised panels, and columns. Smaller objects, such as frames, boxes, and trays, also offer suitable surfaces. The accent table featured here shows faux marble. The look of patterned tiles is created by sectioning off the diamonds with tape before applying a second layer of marble.

MATERIALS

- unfinished wooden table
- sandpaper, assorted grades
- primer
- 2" (50mm) Curve Wide Color Shaper
- soft-bristle wash brush, 1" or 2"
- base-coat color, warm beige (interior latex semigloss paint or fluid acrylic paint)
- glaze colors, light blue, soft green, and deep teal fluid acrylic paint
- glazing liquid
- water-based varnish, satin or semigloss
- painter's tape
- chalk or quilter's pencil
- plastic wrap

Starting Out *Sketch your project to indicate areas to marbleize and to develop a pattern of tiles.*

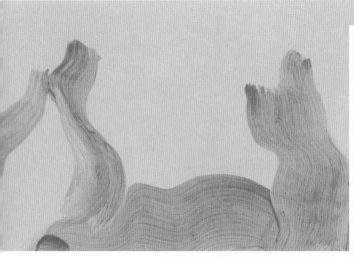

1

2

STEP 1 Follow instructions for preparing wood as directed in the Basic Materials section. Apply base-coat color of warm beige (if you apply a fluid acrylic base coat, seal with one or two coats of varnish). Prepare glazes of light blue and soft green by mixing three parts glazing liquid with one part fluid acrylic paint. Use a soft-bristle wash brush to apply the soft green glaze in diagonal lines. Immediately apply the light blue glaze. With the back of the 2" Curve Wide Color Shaper, gently drag the rounded edge on a diagonal through the wet glaze, softening the two glazes by blending them.

STEP 2 Quickly reverse directions to blend the wet glaze in the opposite diagonal. For a more veined marble effect, carve thin lines into the wet glaze with the corner of the Color Shaper. Dry thoroughly, and seal with a coat of varnish.

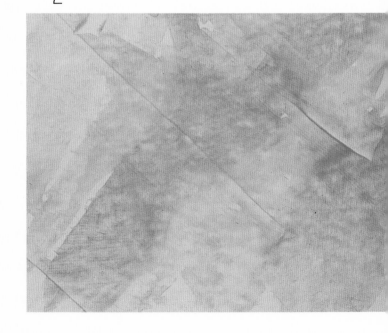

TIP

Apply the deep teal over-glaze in one direction for an even coating. Add a coat of glazing liquid to enhance the transparent qualities of the color.

3

STEP 3 Prepare a glaze by mixing three parts glazing liquid with one part deep teal. Section off a geometric pattern lightly in chalk or quilter's pencil. For a clean-edged tile effect, mask one area at a time with painter's tape. Dip a soft-bristle wash brush into a minimal amount of deep-teal glaze. Apply it gently and evenly over the designated section. Notice how the marble pattern remains visible. Create a second marble pattern in a single step by adding veins, or lines. Apply plastic wrap over the wet glaze, press it gently, and immediately peel it off. Dry thoroughly, and follow the finishing instructions in the Basic Materials section.

before

after

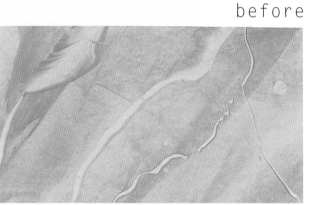

V A R I A T I O N *Experiment with other over-glaze colors during the second marbling process.*

Complete the first marble pattern as directed. Prepare a glaze by mixing three parts glazing liquid with one part light rust. Follow the same procedure as directed in step 3, sectioning and masking for a tile effect. Experiment with color combinations for two-color tile effects.

CUPBOARD

Small accent pieces of furniture have many suitable surfaces for graining techniques. This painted cupboard illustrates the whimsical look possible with graining. Just combine simple color-shaping techniques with your imagination. Traditional American folk art, for example, often incorporates fanciful graining with representational figures, such as animals and birds, to form exuberant patterns.

MATERIALS

- unfinished wood cupboard
- sandpaper, assorted grades
- primer
- 2" (50mm) Decorator Color Shaper (can substitute other sizes or combine several widths)
- 2" soft-bristle wash brush
- base-coat color, antique white (interior latex semigloss paint)
- glaze color, soft periwinkle-blue fluid acrylic paint
- glazing liquid
- water-based varnish, satin or semigloss

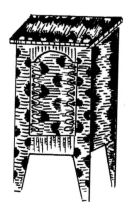

Starting Out *Sketch your project to develop a repetitive pattern over the entire cupboard.*

1

2

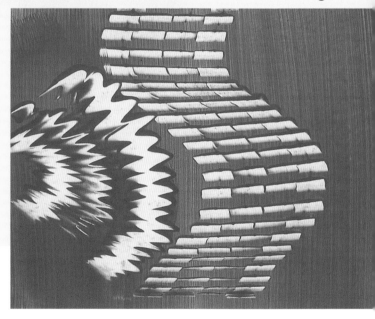

3

STEP 1 Prepare wood as directed in the Basic Materials section. Apply a base coat of antique white to the cupboard (if you use acrylic paint for the base coat, seal the paint with two coats of semigloss varnish). Dry thoroughly. Prepare a glaze by mixing three parts glazing liquid with one part soft periwinkle-blue.

STEP 2 Apply the glaze with the soft-bristle wash brush to one area of the cupboard at a time so that you can work while the glaze is still wet. Add a linear pattern by immediately tapping the 2" Decorator Color Shaper against the surface of the wet glaze. Move down the center to create a wavy line through the wet glaze.

STEP 3 Form zigzag half-circles within the arched areas of the wavy line, working with the 2" Decorator Color Shaper while the glaze is still wet.

4

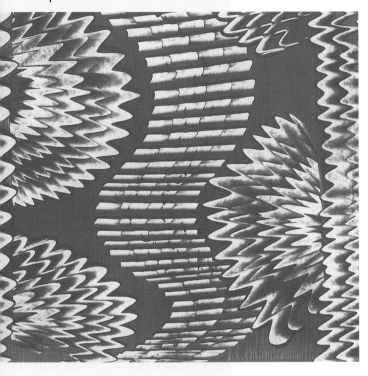

STEP 4 Finish the side with a zigzag stripe. Repeat this pattern on the remaining side, top, and front of the cupboard, modifying as needed for each area's shape and size. Dry thoroughly, and follow the finishing instructions in the Basic Materials section.

TIP

Experiment with the zigzag repetition and half-circle on prepared sample boards. Accomplish the half-circle in one step by moving your wrist freely as you manipulate the Color Shaper.

1

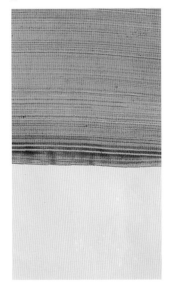

2

VARIATION   *Experiment with graining patterns that use earthy tones.*

STEP 1 Apply a base coat of soft yellow-ochre. Dry thoroughly. Prepare a glaze by mixing three parts glazing liquid with one part burnt sienna. Apply the glaze with a soft-bristle wash brush.

STEP 2 Follow steps 2 through 4 from the original project to complete the effect.

KILIM FLOORCLOTH

Kilims are woven carpets made from cotton or wool and are produced in the Middle East and eastern Europe. Kilims often have geometric patterns, such as squares, diamonds, and checks. This look works well in both traditional and contemporary settings. Floorcloth (heavy-weight canvas made specifically for floors) is well suited to a faux kilim effect. Combine color-shaping techniques with creative thinking to interpret kilim patterns, simulating the flat woven textile.

MATERIALS

- primed canvas floorcloth (this project features a 2′ x 3′ mat; you may wish to explore other sizes or try canvas place mats first)
- 3" (77mm) Curve Color Shaper, cut, notched, and slit (see diagram)
- 1 ½" (38mm) Curve Color Shaper, cut, notched, and slit (see diagram; you can experiment with other sizes and cuts)
- soft-bristle wash brush, 1" or 2"
- base-coat color, light-golden terra-cotta (interior latex semigloss paint or fluid acrylic paint)
- glaze colors, red-orange and light yellow-orange fluid acrylic paint
- stamp color, rustic red fluid acrylic paint
- glazing liquid
- water-based varnish, satin or semigloss
- triangular foam block (can substitute a kitchen sponge, cut into a triangle)

3" (77mm) Curve Color Shaper, cut, notched, and slit

1 ½" (38mm) Curve Color Shaper, cut, notched, and slit

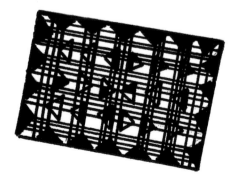

Starting Out *Develop a design on paper first. Refer to traditional kilim patterns, and then experiment with repetitive patterning consisting of geometric shapes.*

STEP 1 Apply base coat of light-golden terra-cotta to primed canvas floorcloth. Do not varnish; stamping techniques work best on an unvarnished surface. Apply rustic red (no glaze added) directly to the foam triangle, and stamp a repetitive triangular pattern on the canvas. Load paint for each stamping, making certain there is no excess around the edges. The illustration shows a simple geometric arrangement. You may wish to experiment with alternative patterns and refer to your sketch as you stamp. Dry thoroughly, and seal with two coats of varnish.

STEP 2 Prepare a glaze by mixing three parts glazing liquid with one part red-orange. Use a soft-bristle wash brush to apply glaze in vertical sections. Immediately pull the 3" Curve Color Shaper, cut, notched, and slit, vertically through the wet glaze to form stripes. Continue this process until the entire floorcloth is covered. Dry thoroughly, and seal with a coat of varnish.

TIP

Wipe the wet glaze from the Color Shaper as you use it.

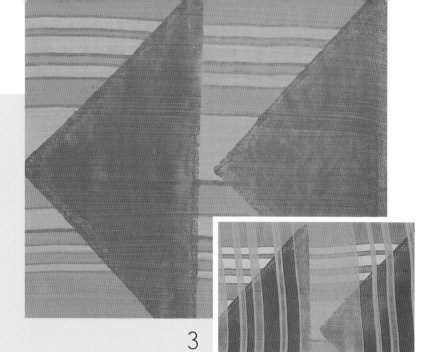

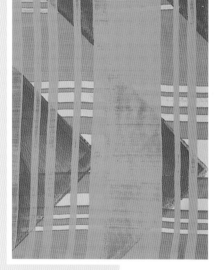

3

STEP 3 Prepare a glaze by mixing three parts glazing liquid with one part light yellow-orange. Use a soft-bristle wash brush to apply glaze over the striped background in horizontal sections. Immediately pull the 1 1/2" Curve Color Shaper, cut, notched, and slit, horizontally through the wet glaze to form stripes. Notice the transparent effects and the patterning that result from layering glazes and color shaping. Apply four to five coats of varnish to produce a functional surface.

VARIATION *Take this pattern to another level by adding a border effect. Simply apply a band of wine glaze around the perimeter of the floorcloth. Notice the rich color changes.*

Seal finished floorcloth with one coat of varnish. Dry thoroughly. Determine the width of the border beforehand, measuring and marking with a quilter's pen. Mask the lines with painter's tape for a clean-edged effect. Prepare a glaze by mixing three parts glazing liquid with one part wine. Apply the glaze, skimming lightly so as not to create puddles. Dry thoroughly, and finish as directed in step 3.

WALLPAPER BORDER

This decorative paper border features a repetitive S-stroke design with horizontal stripes. It was inspired by classical imagery and is created with a soft palette. The result is a simple yet strong pattern.

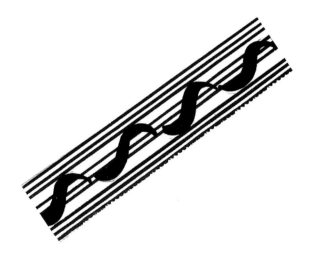

Starting Out *See if you can draw from a simple design element in your surroundings, perhaps a motif from the carpet, draperies, or upholstery. Sketch your design on paper, repeating it to form a pattern.*

MATERIALS

- roll of wallpaper border, plain white (you can measure and cut a border from a roll of plain wallpaper)
- 1" (25mm) Flat Color Shaper
- 1 1/2" (38mm) Curve Color Shaper, cut and notched (see diagram)
- soft-bristle wash brush, 1" or 2"
- base-coat colors, sandy beige and light moss-green (interior latex semigloss paint or fluid acrylic paint)
- glaze color, light teal fluid acrylic paint
- glazing liquid
- water-based varnish, satin or semigloss
- painter's tape
- ruler
- quilter's pencil

1 1/2" (38mm) Curve Color Shaper, cut and notched

1

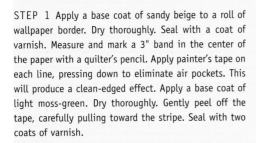

STEP 1 Apply a base coat of sandy beige to a roll of wallpaper border. Dry thoroughly. Seal with a coat of varnish. Measure and mark a 3" band in the center of the paper with a quilter's pencil. Apply painter's tape on each line, pressing down to eliminate air pockets. This will produce a clean-edged effect. Apply a base coat of light moss-green. Dry thoroughly. Gently peel off the tape, carefully pulling toward the stripe. Seal with two coats of varnish.

STEP 2 Due to the length of the border, it is necessary to approach it in sections. Measure 3" lengths, and tape off each section. Complete one section at a time. Prepare a glaze by mixing three parts glazing liquid with one part light teal. Use a soft-bristle wash brush to apply the glaze evenly over the entire sectioned area. Use the 1 1/2" Curve Color Shaper, cut and notched, to pull a stripe through the center of the green band. You can use a ruler to line up the Color Shaper; just smooth out the glaze where the ruler touched it.

STEP 3 While the glaze is still wet, consistently draw S-strokes with the 1" Flat Color Shaper right through the stripe, forming a repetitive pattern.

2

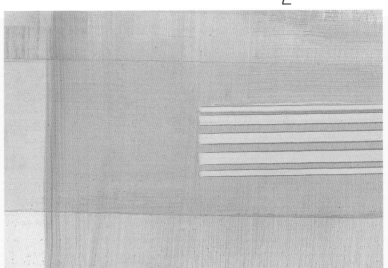

3

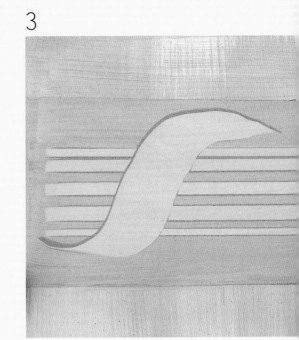

TIP

Practice the S-stroke on palette paper first to get a feel for the stroke and to organize the spacing for the pattern.

4

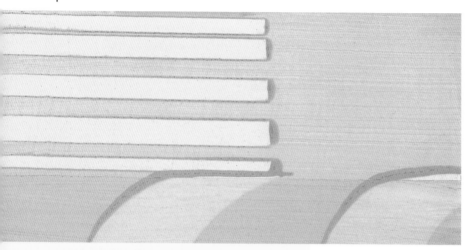

STEP 4 While the glaze is still wet, use the 1 1/2" Curve Color Shaper, cut and notched, to create a parallel stripe at the top and bottom of the pattern. Use a ruler as a guide. Dry overnight, and apply a coat of varnish.

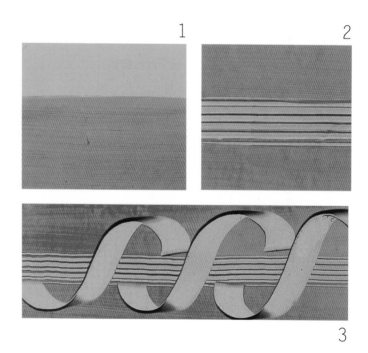

1

2

3

VARIATION *Try a simplified approach, using a two-color combination. This pattern uses a light and dark terra-cotta palette.*

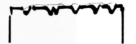

STEP 1 Apply a base coat of light terra-cotta to the wallpaper border. Dry thoroughly, and seal with two coats of varnish. Section off, using the directions from step 2 of the original project.

STEP 2 Prepare a glaze by mixing three parts glazing liquid to one part dark terra-cotta. Follow the same approach as described in step 2 of the original project, creating a striped band in the center of the border. This pattern was created with a 1" Curve Color Shaper, cut and notched.

STEP 3 Use the 1" Flat Color Shaper to make the S-stroke pattern, right through the stripe. Dry overnight, and apply a coat of varnish.

WALL PATTERN

This form shows a stylized, floral design, repeated to produce an overall pattern. A linear flower is created with the 1 ¹/₂" Flat Color Shaper, cut and notched. The Flat Color Shaper makes calligraphic strokes easy, but a Curve Color Shaper also works well. Add subtle texture to the background, using plastic wrap, to soften the effect.

MATERIALS

- primed wall
- 1 ¹/₂" (38mm) Flat Color Shaper, cut and notched (see diagram)
- roller or wall wash brush
- wide soft-bristle wash brush
- base-coat color, light sandstone (interior latex semigloss paint)
- glaze colors, light yellow-ochre and marigold yellow fluid acrylic paint
- glazing liquid (large quantity if for the entire room)
- water-based varnish, satin or semigloss
- plastic wrap
- newspaper or scrap paper

1 ¹/₂" (38mm) Flat Color Shaper, cut and notched

Starting Out *Sketch a few ideas and organize your design on a sheet of paper. Experiment with different placements, perhaps using a random, tossed effect or lining up each flower in a set direction. It will be easier to approach the project if you know the format of your design.*

1

2

STEP 1 Apply a base coat of light sandstone with a roller or wall brush to the wall. Dry overnight. (Varnishing is not necessary.) Prepare a glaze by mixing three parts glazing liquid to one part light yellow-ochre (mix a large quantity for the entire project, and store it in a sealed container). Use the wide, soft-bristle wash brush to apply the glaze in sections. Cut a long strip of plastic wrap, and roll it into a ball. Press the plastic ball into the wet glaze to form a wrinkled pattern. Blot the plastic (on newspaper or scrap paper) as you go along to remove excess glaze trapped in its crevices. Dry overnight. Seal with two coats of varnish.

STEP 2 Prepare a glaze by mixing three parts glazing liquid with one part marigold yellow, also in a large quantity. Use a wide, soft-bristle wash brush to apply the glaze in sections. Create a flower and leaf motif with the 1 1/2" Flat Color Shaper, cut and notched. The flower is made up of a series of curved strokes, for a scalloped effect. The leaf is a simple S-stroke. (Practice on palette paper first.) Continue applying glaze and color shaping in sections until the project is complete. Dry overnight. Apply a coat of water-based varnish.

TIP

To achieve a smooth transition when glazing large areas, try moistening the edges of the wet glaze with a damp sponge as you go along. This will make it easy to join the next section without leaving a line of demarcation.

VARIATION

This pattern works well with brightly colored palettes, as seen in the featured project. It's also effective in more subdued tones. This variation shows a simplified approach using a combination of mint green and soft teal, without an underlay of texture.

STEP 1 Apply a base coat of mint green to the wall. Dry overnight, and seal with two coats of varnish. Prepare a glaze by mixing three parts glazing liquid with one part soft teal. Follow step 2 from the original project to create and complete the pattern.

chrome spiral canister

Containers are perfect first projects and come in lots of interesting forms. The simple lines and small size of this canister make it easy to work with and complement the repetitive, allover spiral design.

Starting Out

You may want to prepare a simple sketch to arrange the design elements or you may wish to be spontaneous and just start to paint.

Remember, the advantage of a metal surface is that you can try different glazing and shaping techniques without harming the background. Simply rinse off the glaze and begin again!

materials

chrome drum container

#2 and #6 Flat Chisel Color Shapers

1"(3 cm) wash brush

turquoise flow acrylic paint

water-based extender

spray acrylic varnish

{1}

Prepare a glaze by mixing one part turquoise flow acrylic paint with one part extender. Using the wash brush, apply the glaze to the chrome surface in sections.

{2}

Work on the "body" of the container first, then the lid. With the #6 Flat Chisel Color Shaper, shape spiral designs randomly into wet glaze. The spirals shown are made with three nested crescent strokes.

{3}

Make simple stripes in a circle on the lid by shaping the wet glaze with the #6 Flat Chisel Color Shaper. Wipe the Color Shaper every few stripes to keep glaze from building up on the tip. Keep the stripes the same length and evenly spaced.

{4}

Create a spiral border on the outside edges of the lid by using the #2 Flat Chisel Color Shaper. The "end" of each spiral should point down toward the bottom of the container. Or for a more "active" design, alternate the spirals so that every other spiral points upward. Seal with varnish.

glaze tip

If you find that the glaze is beading up, try gently sanding the project with #600 wet or dry sandpaper. The slightly rougher surface will help the paint adhere.

variation

Once you have completed the project, you may wish to explore other simple motifs. This reverse curve stroke is done with the #6 Flat Chisel Color Shaper and forms a random pattern.

{1}

Prepare a glaze by mixing one part fuchsia flow acrylic paint with one part extender. Using the wash brush, apply the glaze to the chrome surface in sections.

{2}

With a #6 Flat Chisel Color Shaper, carve a spiral with a long *S* curve ending in another spiral, as shown. The beginning of the spiral may be two separate strokes, but try to make the *S* curve with a single, fluid motion. Seal completed pattern with varnish.

sunflower metal lampshade

Old and new metal lamps can be found in a variety of styles. This particular lamp, which was purchased in bright green, came in an assortment of colors—all of them perfectly suitable backgrounds for Color Shaping techniques. With a light source behind it, this pattern will be especially lovely.

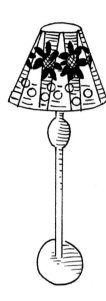

Starting Out

Sketch your ideas on paper to determine the number of flowers for the size of the lampshade.

Use equal spacing when laying out the pattern to avoid running out of room when forming the last flower.

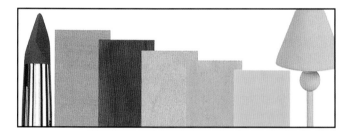

materials

metal lamp

#6 Angle Chisel Color Shaper

1" (3 cm) wash brush

#12 flat shader brush

#4 script liner (or narrow brush of your choice)

flow acrylic paint in yellow-orange,

light magenta, light blue-violet, coral,

and grape

rubber stoppers or corks for printing circles

water-based extender

spray acrylic varnish

{1}

Using the wash brush, paint vertical stripes in yellow-orange around the lampshade. (Note that the green here is the color of the lamp purchased; yours may differ.)

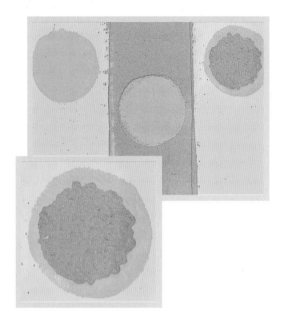

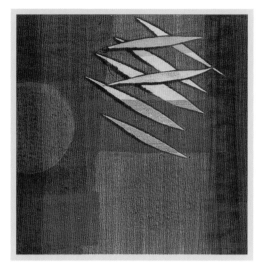

glaze tip

When applying glaze in sections, do not overlap wet glaze over dry glaze. This will create an uneven effect. Instead, try to line up each section of glaze right next to the previous one.

{2}

Apply coral flow acrylic paint directly to a rubber stopper or cork and stamp over the striped background. Load fresh paint for each impression. Let dry, then stamp smaller light magenta circles directly over larger coral ones in the same manner. Let dry, and seal with a coat of varnish.

{4}

Prepare a glaze by mixing one part grape flow acrylic paint with one part extender. With the wash brush, apply the glaze in sections over the entire surface of the lampshade. Using the #6 Angle Chisel Color Shaper, make a crisscross center.

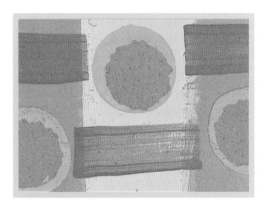

{3}

With the #12 flat shader brush, paint short horizontal strokes in light blue-violet between each of the circles, forming a repetitive pattern. Switch to the #4 script liner or other narrow brush and paint horizontal stripes in coral on the yellow-orange stripes. Let dry. Apply three coats of varnish.

{5}

While the glaze is still wet, shape petals around the center with the #6 Angle Chisel Color Shaper. For the petal stroke, put pressure on the angle edge of the Color Shaper and push away. Let dry thoroughly. Apply four to five coats of varnish to finish the project.

variation

To make an allover pattern on a lampshade, carve a loose scroll or ribbon stroke, accented by black *V*s.

{1}

With the wash brush, paint vertical lilac stripes around the lampshade. Using the #12 flat shader brush, paint horizontal light orange stripes over the first set of stripes, forming a plaid. Let dry. (You may wish to seal this step with a coat of varnish.) With the #4 script liner or another narrow brush, paint vertical stripes spaced evenly over the background (use your eye to judge the spacing). Let dry and seal with three coats of varnish.

{2}

Prepare a glaze by mixing one part light purple flow acrylic paint with one part extender. With the wash brush, apply the glaze in sections. With the #6 Flat Chisel Color Shaper, carve a scroll stroke. The image looks like an inverted *J* motif. Apply a coat of varnish. Using a medium-point indelible black marker, form *V*s in the negative space of the design. Finish with varnish.

rings & checks candlestick

Wooden candleholders can be found in styles ranging from traditional to contemporary. This particular example is broad-based and allows plenty of room for surface decorating. If the candleholder you choose is narrower, experiment with smaller motifs for its design.

Starting Out

Because it is more difficult to "erase" an unwanted stroke on wood than it is on metal, plan the design by creating a simple line drawing.

Use your design to create a clear picture for spacing and repeating shapes.

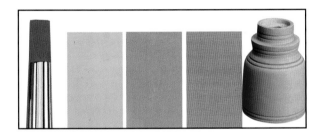

materials

unfinished wooden candleholder

primer

#6 Flat Chisel Color Shaper

1" (3 cm) wash brush

flow acrylic paint in lime green,

   light magenta, and red-orange

water-based extender

water-based varnish

sandpaper in assorted grades

{1}

Prepare wood surface using lime green as the basecoat color. Seal with a coat of varnish.

{2}

Create a checkerboard pattern by painting squares with the wash brush in light magenta. Practice a few times on palette paper to achieve equal sizes and spaces. Paint the trim colors at this time. Seal with three coats of varnish before proceeding.

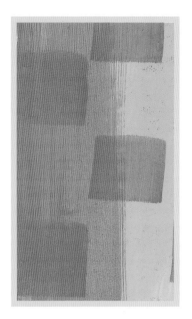

{3}

Prepare a glaze by mixing one part red-orange flow acrylic paint with one part extender. Using the wash brush, apply the glaze in sections in a vertical direction.

{4}

With the #6 Flat Chisel Color Shaper, shape doughnuts into the wet glaze, forming an overall pattern. Notice the interesting design that is created. Dry thoroughly and proceed with the finishing process as directed in the Basic Materials section on page 137.

spacing tip

Use the width of the brush as a guide for the spacing for the checkerboard; a simple brushstroke will create the check.

variation

Experiment with a variety of color combinations, again using the check pattern as the underlayer. Glazing on top with transparent color can create some pleasing color changes.

{1}

Following wood preparation directions, prepare a sea aqua background. Seal this step with a coat of varnish. Then, follow step 2 from the wooden candleholder project using yellow-orange flow acrylic paint.

{2}

Prepare a glaze by mixing one part hot pink flow acrylic paint with one part extender. Using the wash brush, apply the glaze in sections in a vertical direction. With a #10 Cup Chisel Color Shaper (you may wish to experiment with other sizes and shapes), form stripes and zigzags in a vertical direction into the wet glaze. Varnish and finish as directed.

zigzag picture frame

Frames make great projects, whether you choose to insert a mirror or a favorite photo. A painted frame could serve as an extension to a painting with some creative thinking; the range of sizes and shapes is unlimited. Look for a frame that is fairly wide to allow for more surface decoration. The *V*s in this design accentuate the geometric shape of the object.

Starting Out

It is always a good idea to sketch your design on paper first.

Give careful consideration to designs that involve a right angle. Notice how half of the V shape anchors the four corners of the frame.

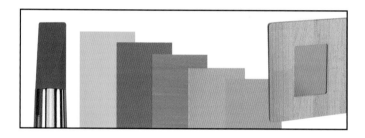

materials

unfinished wooden frame

primer

#10 Flat Chisel Color Shaper

1" (3 cm) wash brush

#12 flat shader brush

flow acrylic paint in yellow ochre,
  light rust, pink, grape, and turquoise

rubber or foam circles for stamping

water-based extender

water-based varnish

sandpaper in assorted grades

{1}

Prepare wood surface as directed, using yellow ochre as the base color. Seal with a coat of varnish. Paint 1" (3 cm) stripes horizontally and vertically with the wash brush in light rust flow acrylic paint. Cover all sides of the frame. Try to match the placement of the stripes to create a symmetrical layout. Seal with a coat of varnish.

design tip

After anchoring the four
corners with the first set of
strokes, complete those **V**s
before continuing to shape
the remaining **V**s. This will
help to distribute the
design evenly.

{2}

Apply pink flow acrylic paint
directly to rubber or foam circles
with the #12 flat shader brush and
stamp on the prepared background.
Load the paint neatly for each
impression. Create an overall pattern
with a random, tossed effect. Seal
with another coat of varnish.

{3}

Continue in the same manner of
stamping, using a smaller circular
stamp with grape flow acrylic paint.
Some overlap adds interest to the
design. Seal this step with three
coats of varnish.

{5}

With the #10 Flat Chisel Color
Shaper, shape *V*s on all sides of the
frame in alternating directions. Begin
by forming half of the *V* in each of
the four corners. This will establish
a guideline. Use firm pressure and
control the straight edges of the
strokes for consistent shapes.
Continue completing the *V*
patterning until all four sections
are shaped. Finish as directed in the
Basic Materials section on page 137.

{4}

Prepare a glaze by mixing one part
turquoise flow acrylic paint with one
part extender. Using the wash brush,
apply the glaze to the prepared frame
in sections.

variation

Try an alternative approach by using a white background and substituting a *U* shape for the *V* shape.

{1}

Prepare a white background and varnish to seal. Apply spring green flow acrylic paint to a rubber or foam circle and stamp all over surface. Apply a coat of varnish. Cover a small rubber circle with blue flow acrylic paint; stamp, overlapping some of the green circles. Apply three coats of varnish to seal.

{2}

Prepare a glaze by mixing one part grape flow acrylic paint with one part extender. Using the wash brush, apply the glaze to wood surface in sections. With the #10 Flat Chisel Color Shaper, carve *U* shapes into the wet glaze. Finish as directed.

leaf motif
box

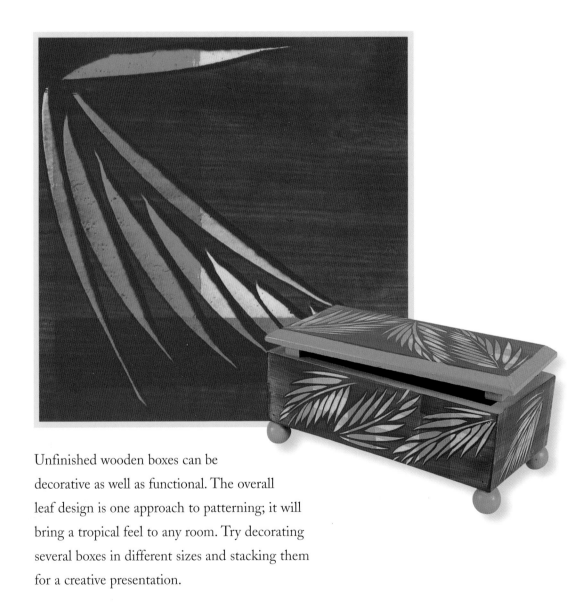

Unfinished wooden boxes can be
decorative as well as functional. The overall
leaf design is one approach to patterning; it will
bring a tropical feel to any room. Try decorating
several boxes in different sizes and stacking them
for a creative presentation.

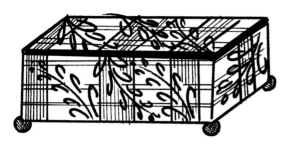

Starting Out

Prepare a simple sketch to arrange the leaves.

Practice making leaf shapes on palette paper with the Angle Chisel Color Shaper.

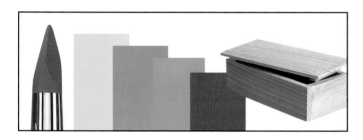

materials

unfinished wooden box

primer

#10 Angle Chisel Color Shaper

1" (3 cm) wash brush

#12 flat shader brush

flow acrylic paint in yellow, turquoise,

   spring green, and wine

water-based extender

water-based varnish

sandpaper in assorted grades

{1}

Prepare wood surface using yellow as the basecoat. Be certain to apply a layer of varnish after the final yellow coat is applied. Next, apply the plaid background by painting evenly spaced, vertical turquoise stripes with the wash brush on the top and sides of the box. You might want to establish the center stripe first, then continue to stripe accordingly. Apply a coat of varnish to seal.

color tip

Select a harmonious color to accent the trim; in this case, turquoise paint was applied. Painted turquoise wooden balls were glued to the box's underside to create feet.

{2}

Using the #12 flat shader brush, paint a series of horizontal green stripes over the turquoise ones, creating a layered effect. This step completes the plaid background. Apply three coats of varnish. Each coat must be thoroughly dry before applying the next.

{3}

Prepare a glaze by mixing one part wine flow acrylic paint with one part extender. Using the wash brush, apply the glaze over the plaid background.

{4}

With the #10 Angle Chisel Color Shaper, establish the center vein of the leaf and then form leafy strokes on both sides of it, starting from the bottom up; the angle of the tip creates the shape of the leaf. Use even pressure. When the pattern is complete, finish as directed.

variation

Experiment with a variety of plaid backgrounds and glazes to form new and interesting designs. The same fern pattern used on the wooden box was re-created here using different colors.

{1}

Prepare a yellow background (follow wood preparation instructions). Apply vertical lavender stripes using the wash brush, letting the width of the brush form the stripe. Seal with a coat of varnish. Paint ¹/₂" (1 cm) horizontal turquoise stripes over the vertical set, using the #12 flat shader brush. Seal with three coats of varnish.

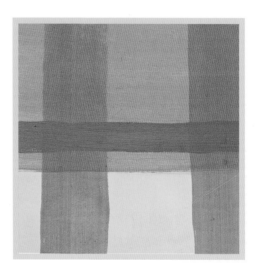

{2}

Prepare a glaze by mixing one part fuchsia flow acrylic paint with one part extender. Using the wash brush, apply the glaze on top of the plaid background in sections. With the #10 Angle Chisel Color Shaper, create the leaves as in step 4 of the wooden box project. Notice the interesting color changes that occur. Finish as directed.

cross band
tray

Unfinished wooden trays can be
found in craft stores, secondhand shops,
or flea markets. They make great painting
projects; this tray's broad, flat surface is ideal
for a large, orderly pattern. Whether used for serving, display,
or organizing smaller objects, they are truly functional.

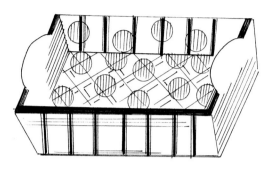

Starting Out

Sketch a design on paper that will complement the shape of the tray.

Prepare the wood as directed on page 137 to ensure the best possible results.

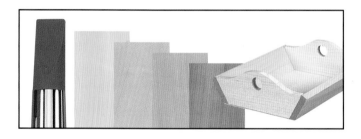

materials

unfinished wooden tray

primer

#10 Flat Chisel Color Shaper

1" (3 cm) wash brush

flow acrylic paint in butterscotch yellow,

    turquoise, lilac, and orange

rubber stopper or cork for stamping

water-based extender

water-based varnish

sandpaper in assorted grades

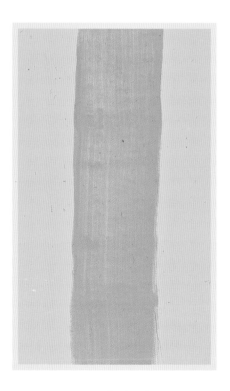

{1}

Prepare a butterscotch yellow background. With the wash brush, paint vertical stripes in turquoise flow acrylic paint, letting the width of the brush form the width of the stripe.

color shaping tip

When Color Shaping the cross band pattern, make long strokes with firm and even pressure. This approach will create a clean image.

{2}

Apply lilac flow acrylic paint directly to a rubber stopper or cork and stamp circles all over the background. For a clear stamped image, apply a fresh coat of paint for each impression. Seal with three coats of varnish.

{3}

Prepare a glaze by mixing one part orange flow acrylic paint with one part extender. With the wash brush, apply the glaze over the entire flat area of the tray.

{4}

While the glaze is wet, use the #10 Flat Chisel Color Shaper to form a cross band pattern. The only way to neatly achieve the crisscross pattern is to do it all at once. You need to work quickly, as there is only so much time before the glaze sets up. Try to space the lines evenly to create a consistent diamond pattern. Finish glazing in orange around the sides of the tray, one section at a time, forming stripes with the Color Shaper. Follow the finishing instructions on page 137 in the Basic Materials section.

variation

Experiment with a variety of cross band designs and stamps, such as this coffee mug holder pattern.

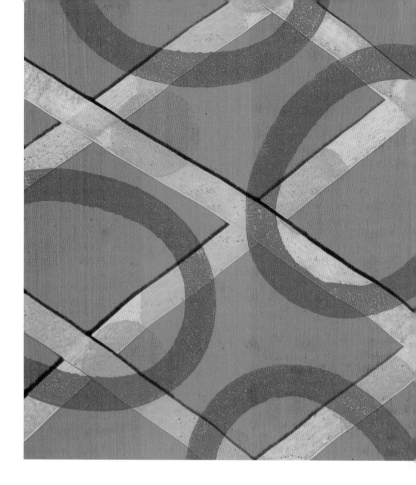

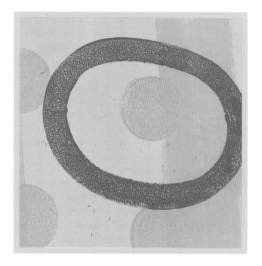

{1}

Prepare a butterscotch yellow background with turquoise stripes and stamped lilac circles as directed in the wooden tray project. Apply purple flow acrylic paint to the opening of a foam coffee mug holder and stamp rings around the circles. Seal with three coats of varnish.

{2}

Prepare a glaze by mixing one part deep teal flow acrylic paint with one part extender. Apply the glaze over the surface as previously directed. Using the #10 Flat Chisel Color Shaper, create the cross band pattern as described in step 4 of the wooden tray project. Refer to the instructions for the finishing process on page 137 in the Basic Materials section.

paper lampshade
designs

Coated paper lampshades have polished surfaces that
work well with Color Shaping techniques. Or, with
some creative planning, Color Shaped patterns can
enhance an already existing lamp base. The playful
design on this lampshade will quickly become a
treasured accent for almost any style of decor.

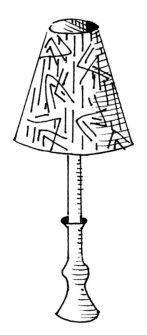

Starting Out

Sketch a few ideas on paper to organize possible design elements.

To see how your design works on a three-dimensional form, bend the paper to simulate the lampshade shape and simply staple it.

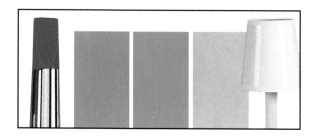

materials

coated paper lampshade

#6 Flat Chisel Color Shaper

1" (3 cm) wash brush

#12 flat shader brush

flow acrylic paint in light magenta, lilac,

   and red-orange

medium-point indelible black marker

water-based extender

water-based varnish or spray acrylic varnish

{1}

With the #12 flat shader brush, paint vertical stripes in light magenta on the lampshade. Seal with a coat of varnish.

varnish tip

On a piece of scrap paper or cardboard, test the marker with a coat of varnish to be certain that no smudging will occur.

{2}

From a diagonal direction, paint short strokes with the #12 flat shader brush in lilac flow acrylic paint, forming an allover pattern. Seal with three coats of varnish.

{4}

You may choose to take the design a step further. Using a medium-point indelible black marker, draw spirals over the Color Shaped pattern. Apply several coats of varnish to seal and protect the lampshade.

{3}

Prepare a glaze by mixing one part red-orange flow acrylic paint with one part extender. With the wash brush, apply the glaze in sections over the prepared background. With the #6 Flat Chisel Color Shaper, create an allover, interlocking *V* pattern. Let dry thoroughly and seal with a coat of varnish.

variation

Experiment with a variety of painted backgrounds and colors, such as this plaid pattern.

{1}

Prepare a plaid background. Paint vertical stripes with the wash brush in golden yellow. Let dry and seal with a coat of varnish. Then paint horizontal stripes in olive green with the wash brush. Let dry and seal with a coat of varnish. Using the #12 flat shader brush, paint vertical stripes in light purple, and seal this step also.

{2}

With a #4 script liner, paint horizontal and vertical stripes in hot pink. The plaid is complete; seal the background pattern with three coats of varnish. Prepare a glaze by mixing one part blue-green flow acrylic paint with one part extender. With the wash brush, apply the glaze in sections and Color Shape *V*s with the #10 Flat Chisel Color Shaper. Seal with varnish.

templates

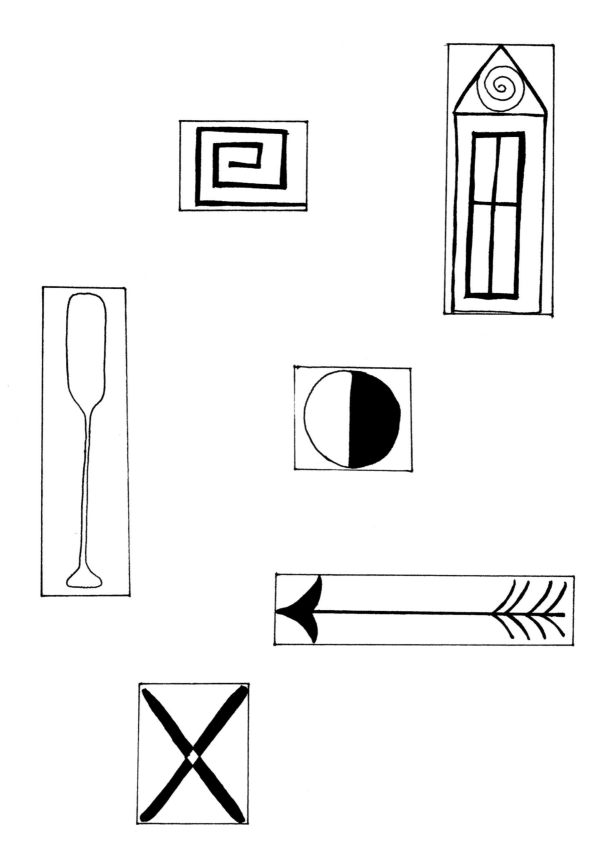

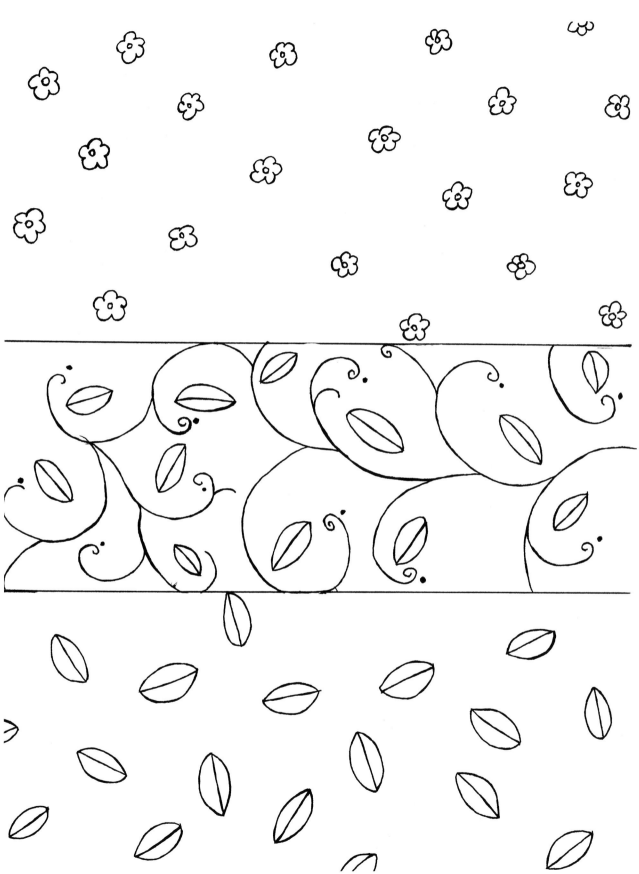

SALT AND PEPPER SHAKERS (PAGS 20–23)

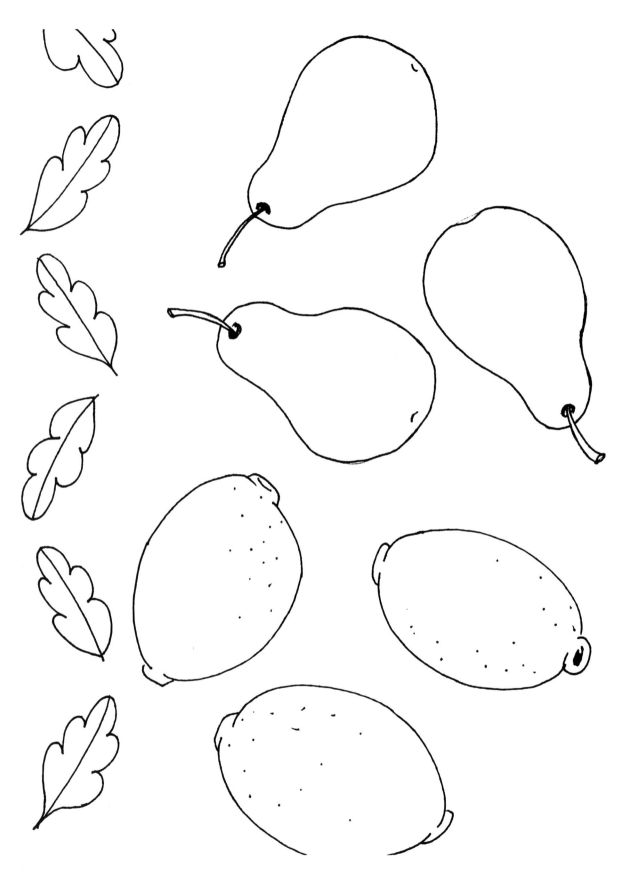

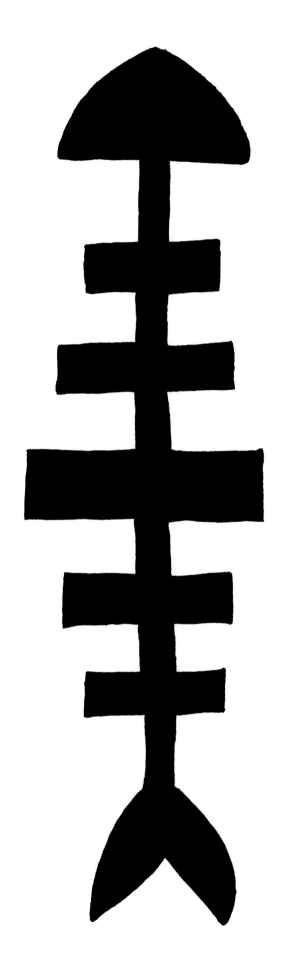

FISHBONE PLATTER (PAGES 44–47)

Fishbone Platter for possible variation (page 47)

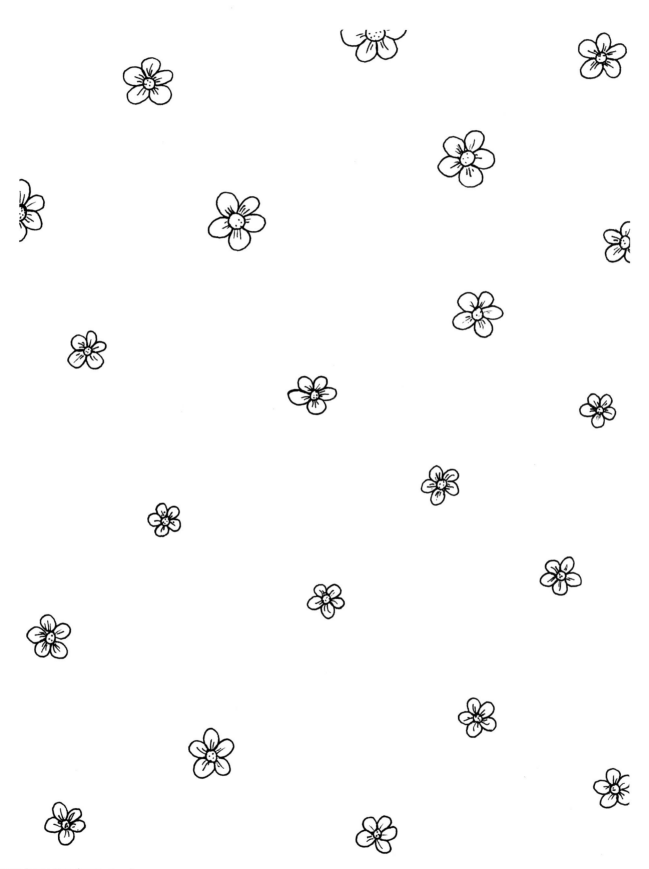

TWO-TONE BOTTLE VASE (PAGES 36–39)

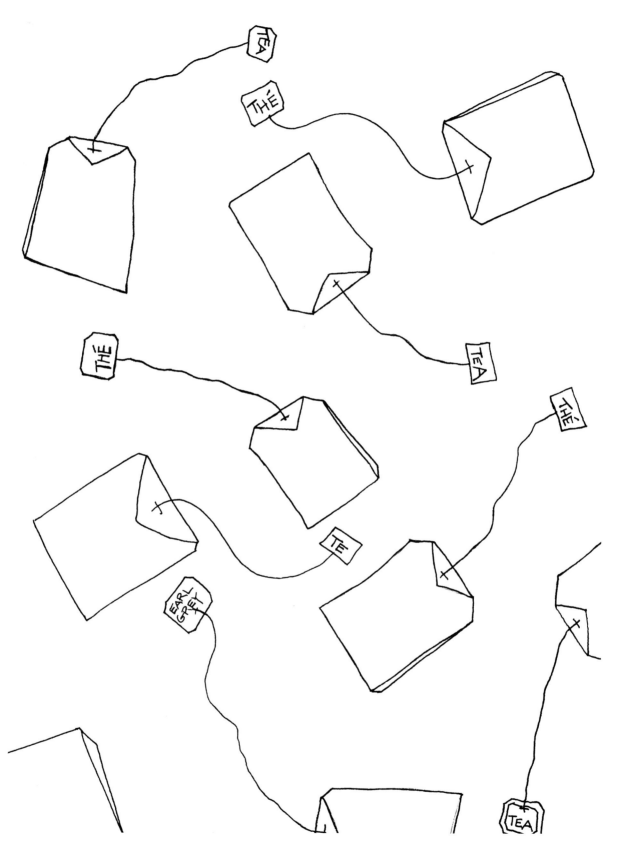

NESTLED TEAPOT AND CUP (PAGES 48–51)

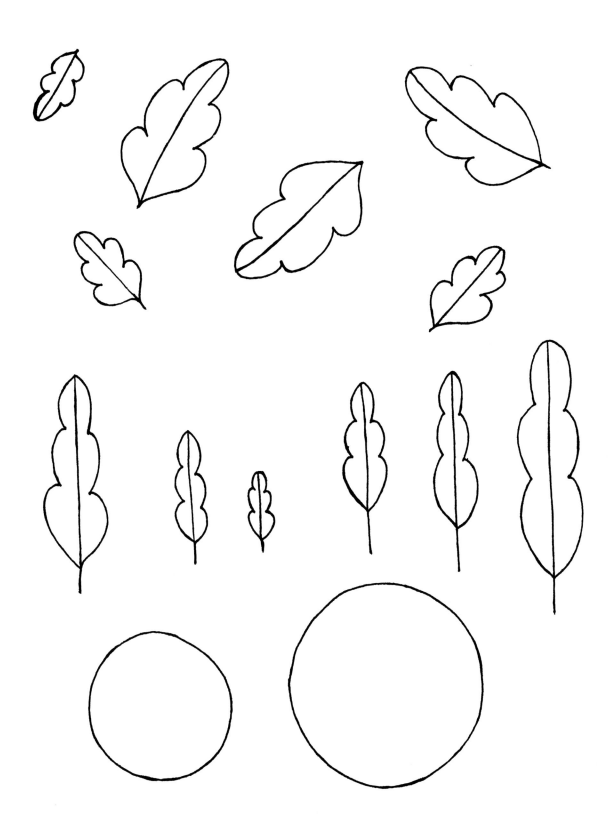

TERRACOTTA PASTA BOWLS VARIATIONS

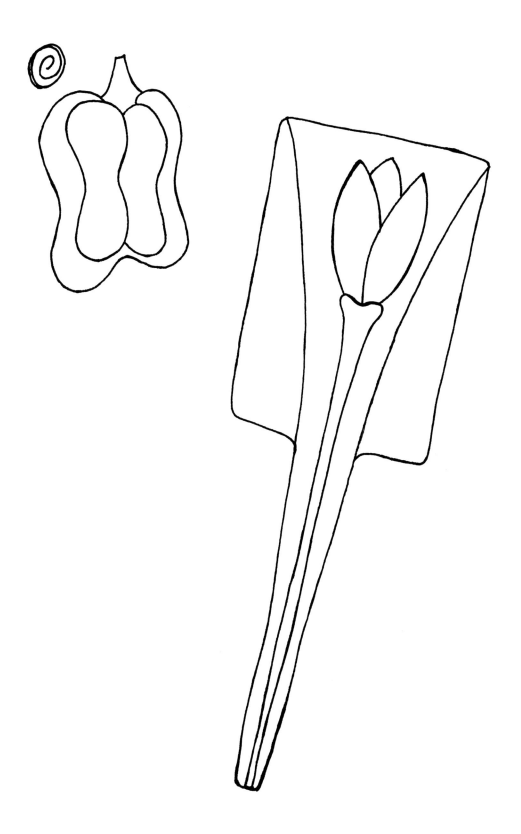

GREEN PEPPER AND TULIP GARDEN MARKERS

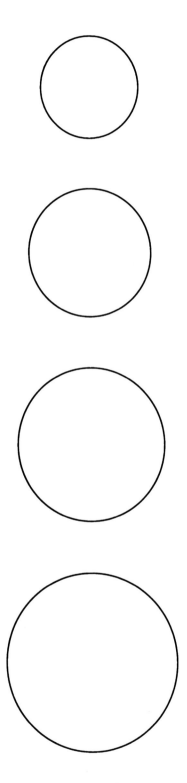

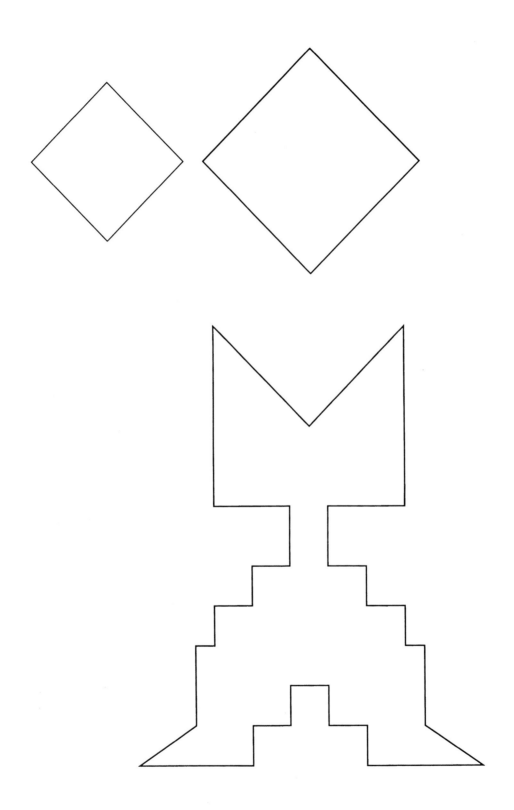

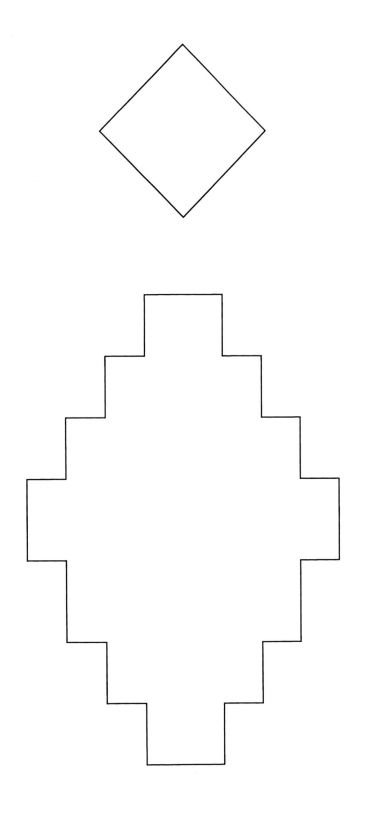

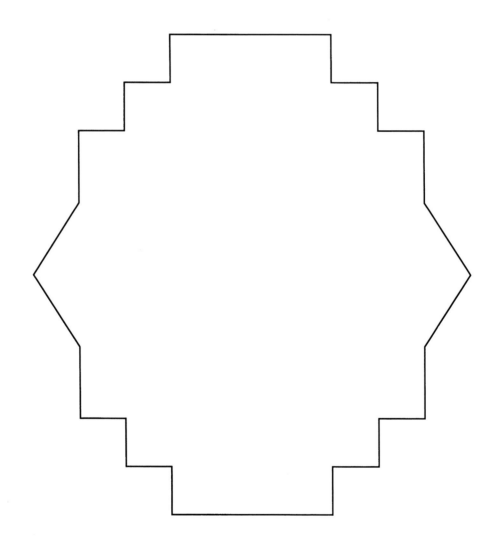

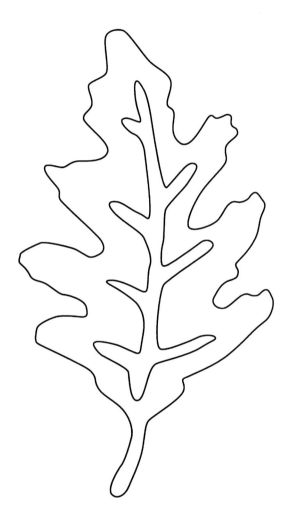

SEVENTIES CHIC VARIATION (PAGE 167) *Make stencils in various sizes for variety.*

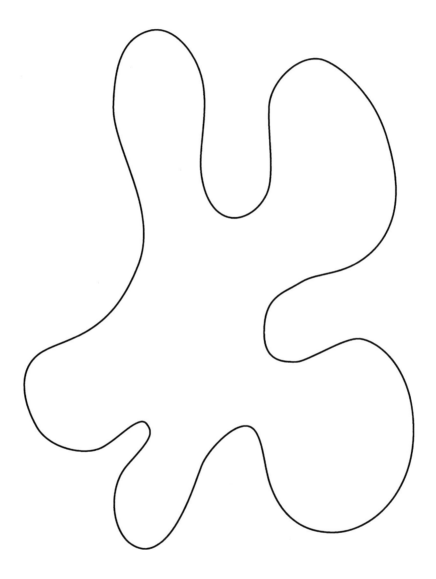

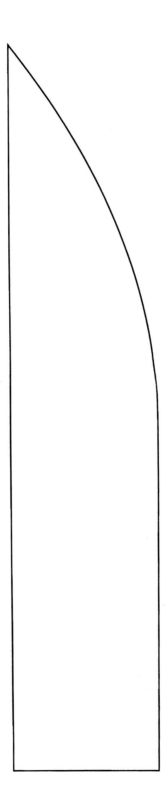

resources

ART SUPPLIES

Corey Ceramic Supply
87 Messina Drive
Braintree, MA 02184
1-800-876-2776

Discount Art Supplies
P.O. Box 1169
Conway, NH 03818
1-800-547-3264
fax (603) 447-3488
www.discountart.com

HobbyCraft
(stores throughout the UK)
Head Office
Bournemouth
United Kingdom
01202-596100

Lou Davis Wholesale
Dept. PC 20, N3211 County Road H
P.O. Box 21
Lake Geneva, WI 53147-0021
1-800-748-7991

Michaels Stores Inc.
8000 Bent Branch
Irving, TX 75063
1-800-MICHAELS
www.michaels.com

National Artcraft
7996 Darrow Road
Twinsburg, OH 44087
1-888-937-2723
www.nationalartcraft.com

Pearl Paint
308 Canal Street
New York, NY 10013
1-800-221-6845
www.pearlpaint.com

Red Barn Ceramics
Route 13 South
Cortland, NY 13045
1-800-640-2039

StenSource International, Inc.
18971 Hess Avenue
Sonora, CA 95370
1-800-642-9293
fax (209) 536-1805
www.stensource.com
*Online catalog for painting stencils

Stencil Craft
www.freespace.virgin.net/stencil.craft
stencil.craft@virgin.net
*Original stencil designs, supplies

COLOR SHAPERS

National Arts Materials
43 Burgess Road
Bayswater
3153 Victoria
Australia
54-1-982-7847
fax: 54-1-981-6225

Oasis Arts & Craft America
Building 2 Unit 1
Homestead Road
Belle Mead, NJ 08502
1-908-874-3315
fax: (908) 874-5433

Royal Sovereign
7 St. Georges Industrial Estate
White Hart Lane
London N22 5QL
United Kingdom
44-181-888-6888
fax: 44-181-888-7029

BISQUEWARE

Art Seasons
667 S. Hudson Avenue
Pasadena, CA 91106
1-888-354-9494
www.artseasons.com

Bisque USA
P.O. Box 23963
Columbus, OH 43223
1-888-247-8729

BMW Bisque
225 Cash Street
Jacksonville, TX 75766
1-800-388-2001
www.bmwbisque.com

Ceramica Imports
60 Spring Street, Suite 414
New York, NY 10012
1-888-424-7533

Garrard Pottery
154 Andrew Drive
Suite 200
Stockbridge, GA 30281
1-880-335-3808
www.garrardpottery.com

PAINT

Behr Process Corporation
3400 West Segerstrom Avenue
Santa Ana, CA 92704
1-800-854-0133
www.behrpaint.com

Benjamin Moore
51 Chestnut Ridge Road
Montvale, NJ 07645
1-800-344-0400
www.benjaminmoore.com
bm@att.net

Gare
165 Rosemount Street
Haverhill, MA 01831
(978) 373-9131
www.gare.com

Glidden
www.gliddenpaints.com

The Home Depot
Consumer Affairs
2455 Paces Ferry Road
Atlanta, GA 30339
(770) 433-8211
www.homedepot.com

Janovic
30-35 Thomson Avenue
Long Island City, NY 11101
1-800-772-4381
fax (718) 784-4564
www.janovic.com

Liberty Design Company
Portsmouth Avenue
Stratham, NH 03885
www.libertydesign.com
*Stenciling supplies, paint, brushes

Martha Stewart Paint
Martha By Mail
11316 North 46th Street
Tampa, FL 33617
1-800-950-7130
www.marthabymail.com
marthabymail@customersvc.com

Mayco/Coloramics Distribution
4077 Weaver Court South
Hilliard, OH 43026
(614) 876-1171
www.mayocolors.com
www.ceramichrome.com

Pratt and Lambert
1-800-BUYPRAT
www.prattandlambert.com

The Sherwin-Williams Company
www.sherwin.com

Spectrum Glazes
P.O. Box 874
Lewiston, NY 14092
1-800-970-1970

FURNITURE
A Big Warehouse
635 West Commerce Street
Gilbert, AZ 85234
1-800-249-4941
www.abigwarehouse.com
info@abigwarehouse.com

Bare Furniture
1680 Riverdale Street
West Springfield, MA 01089
(413) 781-0333
fax (413) 737-2342
www.barefurnitureandreproductions.com
barefurniture@yahoo.com

Country Woods Unfinished Furniture
Outlet
Route 27 (Business Route 101)
Raymond, NH 03077
(603) 895-4118
www.countrywoodsunfinished.com
*Furniture, finishing tips

Crate & Barrel
1860 West Jefferson Avenue
Naperville, IL 60540
1-800-967-6696
www.crateandbarrel.com

Furniture Gallery
1135 Highway One
Lewes, DE 19958
1-888-808-6104
www.furnituregalleryinc.com
furnituregal@ce.net

IKEA
Ikea Catalog Department
185 Discovery Drive
Colmar, PA 18915
1-800-434-IKEA
www.ikea-usa.com

John Lewis
(stores throughout the UK)
Head Office
Oxford Street
London W1A 1EX
United Kingdom
020-7269-7711
www.johnlewis.co.uk

Pop's Unfinished Furniture
8911 Reseda Boulevard
Northridge, CA 91324
1-888-838-0707
818-717-0707
www.popsfurniture.com
popsfurniture@yahoo.com

Selfridges
(stores in London and Manchester, UK)
Head Office
400 Oxford Street
London W1A 1AB
United Kingdom
020-629-1234
www.selfridges.co.uk

Solid Woods, Inc.
40 West Jubal Early Drive
Winchester, VA 22601
(540) 662-0647
fax (540) 662-0672
www.swuf.com
info@swuf.com

Unpainted Furniture City
135 North Broadway
Hicksville, NY 11801
(516) 433-5424

TILES
HBD Ceramics
P.O. Box 910
Leland, MI 49854
(231) 386-7977

index

Paula DeSimone is recognized for her accomplishments in the decorative-arts movement. She is director of the Decorative Painting Certificate Program at Rhode Island School of Design, Continuing Education, In Providence and also teaches courses in decorative arts at the Museum of Fine Arts, Boston, the Fuller Museum of Art, and the DeCordova Museum, all in Massachusetts.

Ms. DeSimone is author of *The Decorative Painter's Color Shaper Book*, *Painting Faux Finishes*, and is co-author with Pat Stewart of *Brush, Sponge, Stamp*, all from Rockport Publishers. She is also featured in her own series of instructional videos, entitled *The Decorative Painter*, produced by Perspective Communications Group, Inc., of Rhode Island. You can visit her Web site at www.thedecorativepainter.com.

Francine Hornberger edits interior design and craft books. She's written for craft product manufacturers and craft book publishers, including the Offray Ribbon Company and McCall's Creates.

Doreen Mastandrea received her MFA from Cranbrook Academy of Art in Michigan. She has taught a variety of courses in ceramics at Salem State College, Montserrat College of Art, the DeCordova Museum, and Mudflat Studios, among others. Her artwork has been shown across the country and in Canada. Currently, Doreen owns Paint A Plate Studio, a paint-your-own pottery show in Lexington, Massachusetts.

Livia McRee is a craft writer and designer who has written and contributed to many books, including *The Crafter's Project Book*, *The Right Light*, *Paper House*, *Quick Crafts*, *Easy Transfers for Any Surface*, the forthcoming *Stained Glass* (all from Rockport Publishers), and *Instant Fabric: Quilted Projects from Your Home Computer* (Martingale & Company).

Virginia Patterson is a fine–arts trained painter. For more than ten years, she has been commissioned to paint everything from traditional canvases to decorative indoor and outdoor murals to unusual objects such as mailboxes, flower boxes, glass pieces, and more. Ms. Patterson regularly restores furniture for interior designers, including stained and upholstery, and has also designed and painted furniture pieces in her original designs. Additionally, Virginia is an accomplished quilter whose work has been exhibited in galleries and art shows across the United States.